D0003122

THE
LONDON
MAPGUIDE
Michael Middleditch

CONTENTS

Congestion Charge Zone see Page 22

All maps in this Mapguide are based on Aerial Photographs supplied by Aerofilms Ltd.
with an original Ground Survey carried out by MICHAEL GRAHAM Publications.

PENGUIN BOOKS

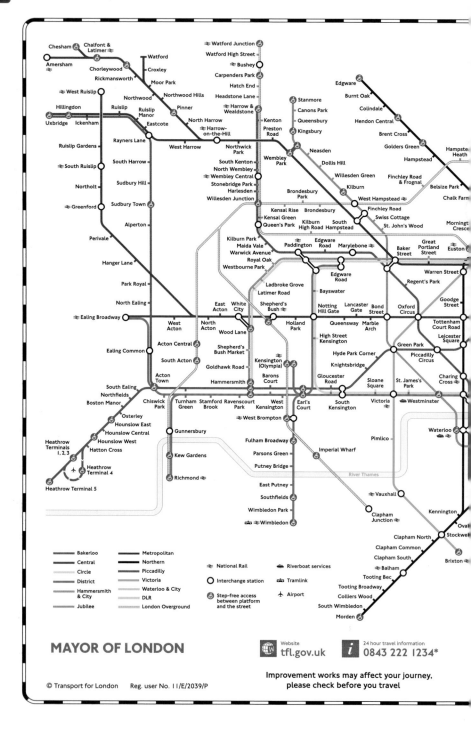

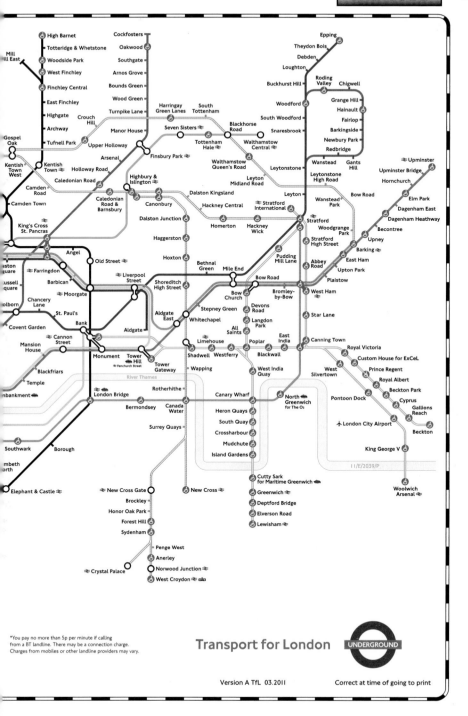

Transport for London

UNDERGROUND

Version A TfL 03.2011

Correct at time of going to print

INTRODUCTION AND HISTORY

A RETROSPECT

I was born in London and spent my early life living in a mundane suburb of London, so it was always a great pleasure for me to escape into Central London. My parents must have felt the same for they delighted in walking my brother and me around the city, always stopping at the statues, and grappling with the history relating to the monuments - Edith Cavell (E5 35) was a favourite. At that time London's sky appeared to be full of barrage balloons and there were even sheep in Hyde Park; the avant-garde dance was the '*jitterbug*' imported by American G.I.'s; and the streets seemed to be full of soldiers and sailors from all the countries in the world.

Probably the most exciting day trip was to the London Zoo. This was an annual event and I keenly looked forward to our leisurely planned walk around the confines of what was then a rather cruel way of keeping animals; but it was nevertheless exciting. We always went as a family to the theatre at least once a year, the Palladium for variety shows, and then after the war to Drury Lane, the Coliseum and the marvellous Stoll Theatre in Kingsway (long since demolished for an office block), where we saw all the great American musicals.

When I reached my 'teens' it was football and cricket and music as well that attracted me to London. I can't believe how many times I saw opera at Covent Garden in a year - prices have gone up! I remember a concert at the Festival Hall sitting behind the massive shoulders of Vaughan Williams. The 100 Club in Oxford Street (which amazingly is still there) and the bebop clubs scattered around Leicester Square were also popular haunts of mine at that time. Another pastime was roaming and rummaging through Foyles and the numerous secondhand book and record shops in Charing Cross Road looking for bargains. Most of my early working life was spent working in Fleet Street…I loved it - the cosy little pubs scattered around the area offering bitter and home-made food (pre-microwave), and perhaps even a glimpse of my favourite newspaper cartoonist. The office I worked in was on Fleet Street so we were able to see the Lord Mayor's parade and all the visiting dignitaries. I remember rushing out into the street to see my hero Yuri Gagarin - hardly anybody was there to see him, so my friend and I got a special wave. In the evenings I walked back to Liverpool Street Station past bomb damage from the war that had not been reconstructed. In later years my steps were quicker as I eagerly looked forward to seeing my wife and our newborn son in the summer months waiting at the station the other end.

LONDON TODAY

There is no doubt London has changed: a certain continental air pervades, people sit on pavements in inclement weather sipping coffee. Covent Garden piazza has thankfuly been preserved - no vegetables but a lively shopping and eating area: Camden Lock is now a young people's preserve with a large market; Soho is no longer full of strip clubs - you are more likely to see men kissing and cuddling in public! The old financial area has been re-invented with a number of interesting and controversial buildings, and a few eyesores; Ludgate railway bridge no longer obscures the view of St. Paul's, though the city area is still as big a hodge-podge as it was in Wren's day! Young people who were born in the suburbs seem now to prefer to live in Central London again, I can understand that…that's life!

THE STREETS OF LONDON

London was no more than a swamp (*Llyn-dyn* in Celtic means a stronghold by the marsh) when the Romans first pitched camp on the northside of the Thames in AD 43, and built their town: it was called *Londinium* and was located between the Tower as it is now, and where the River Fleet used to enter the Thames close by the present Blackfriars Bridge. They built the first wooden bridge across the Thames (at the bisection of the town area) and a stone wall which, if it had been built a century earlier, might have stopped the warrior queen Boudicca from burning the town. Londinium was the heart of the Roman province of *Britannia* and the capital; it had a very large prestigious basilica (a Roman law court building) and forum (market place) which would encompass Gracechurch Street. Like so much of London, the street names tell the story: 'Walbrook' was once a small stream which ran through the centre of the Roman town.

When the legions finally withdrew in AD 410 after the collapse of the Roman Empire, civilization declined; the Walbrook flooded again and the town fell into ruins. For an idea of how London looked then visit the Museum of London (D2 36).

Overrun by Angles, Saxons and Jutes, the British fled westwards to Wales leaving what then became known as *Angleland* (England) to the marauders. Although the invaders were heathens it did not take long before Christianity had gained a footing and churches began to appear: St.Paul's was founded in the year 604 and a monastery was established at Westminster. London's importance only began to recover during the reign (871-901) of King Alfred the Great: he made London habitable again. Alfred built a navy which tussled with

and beat the Danish and Norse pirates who were rampaging continuously up the creeks and rivers. Eventually when peace came the Danes were allowed to settle and Canute became the King - he was also King of Denmark. The Strand (F5 35) - then a suburb of London - and Southwark on the other side of the Thames were Danish enclaves.

FRENCH CONNECTION

Having spent a great deal of his early life in Normandy, Edward the Confessor was enamoured with the Norman style of building, which was an extension of the Romanesque. He established the early palace and abbey at Westminster, where he was crowned. He died in 1066 and the Norsemen or Normans who had adopted the French language arrived and William the Conqueror became King. He built the Tower of London - the White Tower - (see page 53) which still stands today. Probably one of the finest examples of the Norman-style of church building to be seen in the city is the church of St.Bartholomew the Great (C2 36). The French contribution to architecture and in particular to the building of cathedrals with stone roofs gradually culminated in the pointed Gothic style, and with the establishment of English-Gothic architecture.

Today it is difficult to imagine that the Houses of Parliament stand on what was once the small island of Thorney - the site of the early Westminster Abbey which was demolished by King Henry III in 1205, when centuries of construction commenced on the building of the Abbey (E4 43) as we see it now.

MEDIEVAL TIMES

London had become three districts during this period: the City, Westminster and Southwark - which was connected to the

EDITH CAVELL MEMORIAL (E5 31)
'PATRIOTISM IS NOT ENOUGH I MUST HAVE NO HATRED OR BITTERNESS FOR ANYONE'

OLD LONDON BRIDGE BY CLAUDE DE JONGH

city by the old stone London Bridge, which lasted from 1209-1756, and had houses and even a chapel built on top of it. Southwark was renowned for brothels and other entertainments: bull and bear rings were attractions long before Shakespeare's 'Globe' arrived in 1599, and it has returned again, thanks to the years of endeavour by the American actor Sam Wanamaker who finally managed to get the theatre reconstructed close to the original site (D6 36). Westminster housed the royal residence until it finally became the home of Parliament during Henry VIII's reign. Westminster Hall is all that is left to see of this original building if you do visit the Houses of Parliament. In the City the merchants established their guilds and they elected the first mayor of London in 1188; the City has remained autonomous since that time. There were also large priories at Blackfriars and Whitefriars - friars unlike monks were in the beginning working Christians who tended the sick and needy; in *The Canterbury Tales* Chaucer gives another view. Henry VIII banned monks and friars and unfortunately he knocked down many beautiful abbeys and monasteries.

GROWTH - FIRE - PROSPERITY

Towards the end of the Tudor lineage London's population had reached almost 200,000. Henry VIII had laid out Hyde Park and St. James's Park and moved the royal palace to Whitehall, but it was his daughter Elizabeth I who was probably responsible for the growth of the city: she granted the East India Company the monopoly of trade with the eastern hemisphere. This was the beginning of London as a financial centre. After abolishing the monarchy and to a certain degree self-inflicting Oliver Cromwell on themselves, the British people returned to monarchy with restrictions. After centuries of exclusion, Cromwell had allowed Jews to settle in London, and this was certainly good for finances and the country.

In 1666 after a terrible plague, fire broke out destroying most of the city and the old St. Paul's. The phoenix was Christopher Wren (see page 14), whose plan for the city was never allowed to come to fruition as people hastened to rebuild without a great deal of attention to planning. The Monument (G5 37) was designed by Wren and was erected near where the fire started; who could ever dispute the uplift that St Paul's gives to the spirits of Londoners? When the 18th century dawned the Bank of England had been founded for just six years and London had become the largest financial centre in the world, overtaking Amsterdam. Residential districts grew in Lincoln's Inn and Covent Garden, which already had the marvellous Inigo Jones piazza and St. Paul's church. London's famous landmark squares were also laid out as the century proceeded. The trade with the east brought the phenomenon of coffee houses, where business was often transacted.

In 1811 the country had a Prince Regent (later George IV) and a certain architectural style which is attributed to the architect John Nash who was reponsible for one of London's joys - the lovely Cumberland Terrace (H3 25) that overlooks Regent's Park. The Haymarket Theatre (D6 34) and also a

considerable part of Buckingham Palace (A3 42) are attributed to him.

DICKENS' LONDON

London during Queen Victoria's reign was the capital of a huge and much envied empire, and the scene of a great deal of squalor - not a cardboard city then and certainly not as jolly as a Christmas card, but without doubt the inspiration for the art and heart of Charles Dickens. Many of his locations are still very much the same as they were in his day, particularly around the Temple area (H4 35). The River Thames was spanned by most of the bridges we see today and with the advent of the steam engine, railways were constructed enabling London to spread even further afield. The villages of Islington, Hampstead and Highgate were no longer separate, yet strangely if you visit them, a certain amount of village atmosphere still prevails. The central station terminuses were built - St. Pancras (E3 27) is a monument itself to the steam age and is Londons finest station.

Another man who never forgot his roots in Lambeth (A5 44) was Charlie Chaplin whose autobiography vividly describes his life in south London at the end of the 19th century, when music halls and pubs became escapes from the tedium of work. Although many theatres have disappeared there are plenty of pubs to get the feel of life in those days.

MILLENNIUM

By the beginning of the 20th century London's population had reached 6.5 million, larger than Paris and New York. It had spread far and wide due to the underground system that enabled commuters to travel quickly into central London. Unscathed by the Great War, much of the city was destroyed later when the Second World War started. Hitler attempted to demoralize the British people with his 'blitzkreig', which like a tinderbox set London's East End and docks on fire: the red skies of those autumn nights of 1940 are indelible on my memory.

Although reconstruction was slow after the war; the Festival of Britain in 1951 did inaugurate new forms of building and architecture - the Festival Hall is an example of this period. Today within the labyrinth of the city you will discover the amazing and interesting diversity of the architecture - although you cannot always see some features due to the closeness of the building - that is the unique character of the City of London.

However in Canary Wharf (64) and Paddington Basin (A2 32) the best of London's 21st century integrated urban planning shines through.

Try the canal-side walk from the Zoo or Camden market to Little Venice and then on to the Basin where you can take a rest in a restaurant or café and watch the world go by. For a good view over London's roof-tops, walk up Primrose Hill (E1 25). A plaque at the top explains the panorama for you.

A YEAR TO REMEMBER

What a year 1948 was! Palestine became Israel - a religious state, Ghandi was assassinated, South Africa introduced apartheid, and Czechoslovakia became a Soviet satellite.

In 1948 London had hardly picked itself up from the war - austerity and to a certain extent a little of the wartime spirit still prevailed; we were grappling to get on our feet again. For me nothing was too much different, aware of course that we were no longer in danger of a bomb or doodle-bug suddenly dropping on us, and my pre-war life too far off to remember - I had really known nothing else other than austerity! The wartime cameraderie was filtering away and to me it seemed that London was getting meaner and used to the smart, crooked wide shoulder-padded 'spivs', personified by the comedian Arthur English - a forerunner of George Cole's Arthur Daley in the TV series *Minder*. It took another twelve years before the materialistic society at least really got under way. Back in 1948 I was just about completing my first year at grammar school and intensely interested in sport, particularly cricket and football. Suddenly, London was alive again, the Olympic Games had arrived. Some of the competitors still remain in my thoughts: Maureen Gardner, the ballet dancing-teacher, darling of the hurdles; Jack Gardner (no relation) our future heavyweight boxing champion, who was once rated higher than Rocky Marciano; the runners McDonald Bailey (GB) and Arthur Wint, a very popular Jamaican athlete in England where he was studying medicine at London University. I later ran at meetings where the two of them and Roger Bannister - whose best days were later - ran.

The athletes whose achievements stood out most in my memory of the 48 games were: *'The Flying Dutch Housewife'* Fanny Blankers-Koen, who won four gold medals and the amazing Czech long-distance runner Emil Zátopek, who did even better at the next games in Helsinki.

There is no doubt that the greatest drama was at the end of the games - the Marathon. I have never forgotten the moment when the Belgian Étienne Gailly, the first contestant in the race to enter the old Wembley Arena, staggered onto the track: he was absolutely exhausted and was passed by the Argentinian Delfo Cabrera and the Welshman Tom Richards. Finally, and deservedly, he summoned up enough willpower to get the bronze medal.

SOVIET AMATEURISM

The years following the war saw the advent of the state-sponsored athletes in the communist-controlled countries: athletes were given all the facilities and incentives to perfect their skills without having monetary worries. This heralded changes in the 1970s to the strict amateurism rules: commercialization was introduced with world-wide television broadcasts and sponsorship, and the spectacular opening and closing ceremonies. All this puts the Games today on another planet to the Games of 1948. The only live event I saw was water polo in our local swimming pool, Finchley Lido, now a Vue cinema and restaurant site. Anything else I watched, was at the cinema or on our small nine-inch Radio Rental Baird television. That year in the spring about fourteen of us had huddled in front of a minuscule TV to watch the Football Cup Final, Manchester United v Blackpool with the wonderful

twinkled-toed Stanley Matthews playing for the latter: no £220,000 a week for him, I guess in 1948 he would have been lucky to get £12.

SCHOOL SPORTS

As I have said, my sporting interests were with team games, although I often ran at the old White City stadium (now BBC studios) in school athletics, always trying in the 100 yards to get to the All England finals and usually being beaten by Paul, an older runner from my school with strangely short legs for a sprinter, but how he could move them! The year when Paul had moved up into the next category I thought I stood a chance, and was most disappointed when the sports master put me in for the 440 yards: I wrangled with him, all to no avail. He said we think you will do better in this event - and how right he was. He put the best runner in the school in charge of me, to teach me how to run the event. He and

I both went through to the All England Schools Championship sponsored by the *News Chronicle* newspaper at Southampton. We lodged together, in a very large house that was part nursery and was run by a retired army officer - we were asked not to be too noisy in case we disturbed the babies! We were there for three nights during the summer of 1951, Clive was in the seniors and I was in the junior 440 yards. Clive was as usual (he had competed in the All England before) unfortunately running against a future Olympic runner, Derek Johnson, who won the silver medal in the 800 metres at the 1956 Melbourne Olympics. Incidently Johnson, through the Athletes Union, was in direct opposition to Margaret Thatcher when she tried to get our athletes to boycott the 1980 Moscow Games.

Returning to the schoolboy championships, I won all my heats and was drawn in the far outside lane for the final: I was just pipped and came second after leading all the way round on an undulating grass track. Nevertheless I was given the same time as the winner, a new England record for the junior event. I have always said half of that feat I owe to Clive as well as a few pounds he wiped off the slate playing poker! My next event was the following year in the first indoor athletics meeting in this country at Harringay Arena: 600 metres on boards. Never having run this event and jostling on boards, I was lucky to get a medal from the sports commentator Harold Abrahams, whose achievements with the 'Flying Scotsman' Eric Liddell in the 1924 Paris Games were featured in the Academy Award film *Chariots of Fire*. When I saw the film years later I realized that Abrahams had won the 100 metres gold medal, Liddell also won Gold for the 400 metres. Cricket was my first love though and throughout the summer months I practised my bowling in the local park in the evenings. Perhaps the most memorable event was playing for the local schools eleven against a Winchmore Hill team which included the famous West Indian all-rounder, Learie Constantine, who endured racism in the 1940s, and won a famous court case because of this. Playing in our team was future England and Fulham football captain Johnny Haynes, a particular favourite of my father, who had predicted fame for him when he saw him playing for Edmonton Boys. I had a brief spell for this North London football team picked from local

JESSE OWENS was born in Alabama in 1913, a grandson of slaves. Segregation was a way of life in that Southern state, so at the age of nine his parents moved north to Cleveland, Ohio. While attending high school he equalled the world record for the 100 yards. Later he went on to Ohio State University. At the 1936 Berlin games he won four gold medals.

100 metres - 10.3 seconds
He also jointly held the world record 10.2 seconds at that time.
200 metres - 21.1 seconds an Olympic record
He also jointly held the world record 20.3 seconds at that time.
Long jump - 26 feet $5^1/2$ inches, an Olympic record
His world record of 26 feet $8^1/4$ inches lasted for 25 years
4 x 110 metres relay

schools. I went for a trial as a goalkeeper, unfortunately a number of boys turned up for this position, so in order to make up a team, they put me on as a centre forward - totally out of my depth but able to run, I scored a few goals. They told me we do not care what you are like as a goalkeeper you will make centre forward for us. I knew different, and I was right this time. I played just four games and was then dropped. It was not my position, although I managed to train at Tottenham Hotspurs ground during my short spell. The team went on that year to get to the quarter finals of the English Schools Shield, being knocked out by Liverpool Boys. The final was always played at Wembley.

THE MAN FROM ALABAMA

Without question the most memorable sporting meeting I have ever had was in Singapore while doing my National Service in the band of the 15th/19th Hussars in 1955-6. Music at that time had become the most important part of my life. Having passed my music theory exams and endeavouring to play the trumpet, I was given a pass straight through to the band who were based in Ipoh, in what was then Malaya. I had a marvellous time playing music solidly for nearly two years.

During my time abroad I ran in the Malayan Games, changing back into uniform between heats to play my cornet in the band. Then, while spending a month as duty band in Singapore I was doing some research in the library of the American Information Service Office near Collyer Quay. Standing in the room was this tall athletic man, dressed in an immaculate blue suit. Apparently this man had been nominated by President Eisenhower to be the Ambassador of Sport. Somebody then came over to me and asked me whether I would I like to meet him. I was indeed very pleased to meet him..............

I shook hands with a legend, a great athlete and human being, Jesse Owens, the man who upset Adolph Hitler.

MARATHON ROUTE

FOUR CIRCUITS

THREE COMPLETE CIRCUITS

LITTLE BRITAIN
GUILDHALL
WARWICK LANE
BANK OF ENGLAND
CHEAPSIDE STREET
KING STREET
ST PAULS
BOW CHURCH
CORNHILL
LIME STREET PASSAGE
BLACKFRIARS
QUEEN VICTORIA ST.
GRACECHURCH STREET
EMBANKMENT
CANNON ST.
EASTCHEAP
MONUMENT
TOWER HILL
TRAFALGAR SQUARE
CLEOPATRA'S NEEDLE
THAMES
TOWER OF LONDON
THE MALL
GREEN PARK
Finish
Start
ST JAMES'S PARK
VICTORIA
THE MALL START / FINISH
BUCKINGHAM PALACE
BIRDCAGE WALK
BIG BEN
HOUSES OF PARLIAMENT
ONE CIRCUIT

2012

42·195 TOTAL KILOMETRES
26·2 TOTAL MILES

Map reference E2 35 Set in Bloomsbury this is truly a great museum - in the top league with few rivals - and it is the most popular museum in London. This superb building houses an immense collection of treasures from all over the world. It was built in 1857 in the neo-classical style by the architect Robert Smirke, and if you approach the museum from the south, you view a magnificent Ionic-colonnaded façade with a pediment containing allegorical sculptures that represent the progress of the human race in Art and Science etc. The museum was founded in 1753, when physician Sir Hans Sloane's library and varied collection of over 80,000 objects, including plants, fossils, coins and manuscripts, was purchased by the government with proceeds of a public lottery. The first home of the museum was on the present site in a 17th century mansion known as Montague House, which disappeared when the existing building was constructed. The azure, round 'Reading Room' which is absolutely magnificent was finished in 1857 and is the work of Smirke's younger brother Sydney. In the centre of the area - originally an open quadrangle - Smirke built his dome which is over 140 feet in diameter, and is wider than the dome of St.Peters in Rome. With the removal of the 'British Library' to St.Pancras and the beginning of the new century, a glass roof was constructed to span the two acre courtyard and dome, it has been renamed the 'Great Court'.

THE MARVELS OF ATHENS

There is no doubt that the 'Elgin Marbles', are one of the museums greatest attractions, and it is very easy to understand why the Greeks would like to see them returned to Athens. Collected by the Earl of Elgin in 1801, they were sold to the British government in 1816. Originally these sculptures, reckoned by many people to be the greatest classical carvings in the world, adorned the 438 BC Parthenon - the Temple of Athene Parthenos (the virgin) - which overlooks Athens from the Acropolis hill. It is quite likely they would have been broken up if Elgin had not acquired them - who knows? You can view these wonders on the ground floor in the Duveen Gallery, which was purpose built in 1938 to exhibit them.

MADNESS IN GREAT ONES
Staring eyes have always seemed to me to be linked with some form of madness: I think of Hitler, Mosley and other such gangsters. The bust of the Roman emperor Augustus (27BC - AD14) is striking for his piercing eyes inlaid with marble and glass, and his posture. He was not mad though: related to Julius Caeser, he became Rome's first Emperor and set about undoing military dictatorship and making the empire more constitutional. See room 70.

METALLIC BEAUTY
In the centre of room 33 is the 8th century figure of Tara a goddess from Sri Lanka in gilded bronze. The sculpting of material is sheer beauty.

THE MUMMIES OF EGYPT
Children always seem to have a strange fascination for the bandaged mummies inside their exotic cases, and there are rooms full of them to contemplate. I was frightened as a small child (pre-Hammer) when I was taken to the cinema, so I would not be the night watchman in this gallery. Here too, is 'Ginger', a man born over 5000 years ago, who was near as perfectly preserved in hot desert sand - he was given his name because of the colour of his hair.

SUTTON HOO TREASURE
In 1939 the remains of a 7th century ship were accidently found in a Suffolk field. The ship contained the treasures of an Anglo-Saxon king, who had been buried with his worldly acquisitions, including many interesting pieces of jewellery in gold and enamel which are well preserved and worth seeking out. His helmet is really stunning and although once fragmented it has been very carefully restored.

REFLECTION
With such a vast selection you have to make your own choice. Here are a few that might interest you: an amazing 1585 ship clock (the dial is at the foot of the main mast) made in Prague, elegant Chinese porcelain, the Roman 'Lycurgus Cup' in green glass that changes ruby-red in light and with wine, Isle of Lewis 12th century chessmen, Venetian glass, amazing collections of coins, and the 'Rosetta Stone'. Drawings by Dürer, Michelangelo, Watteau, Claude Lorrain, and Turner are not necessarily on display but they can be viewed.
The Museum shop is an ideal place to buy presents or souvenirs to remind you of your visit to London. Prints, scarves, books, jewellery, and replicas of many of the museums sculptures are on sale.
Once inside the museum obtain a museum floor plan; you will need it!

GROUND FLOOR
GREEK & ROMAN
Including Bassae sculpture, the Nereid Monument - Sculptures from the Parthenon.
WESTERN ASIA
Ancient Palestine - Assyrian sculpture - Khorsabad, Nimrud, and Nineveh palace reliefs.
EGYPTIAN SCULPTURE
ORIENTAL COLLECTIONS
China, South and Southeast Asia - Amaravati sculpture - Islamic art.
ETHNOGRAPHY
The Mexican Gallery
THE READING ROOM
BASEMENT
GREEK and ROMAN
Architecture - Greek Sculpture - Ephesus
WESTERN ASIA
Ishtar Temple - Assyrian art.
UPPER FLOORS
PREHISTORIC & ROMANO-BRITISH
Stone Age (mezzanine) - Prehistory - Roman Britain
MEDIEVAL, RENAISSANCE and MODERN
Medieval tiles and pottery - clocks & watches - Waddesdon Bequest -
Europe 15th, 18th, 19th centuries -
Europe & America 20th century.
WESTERN ASIA Ancient Iran, Anatolia - Syria - Nimrud ivories - South Arabia
EGYPT Mummies - Tomb paintings and Papyri - Egypt and Africa - Coptic Egypt.

COINS and MEDALS
GREEK and ROMAN
Rome: City & Empire -
Pre-Roman Italy-
Ancient Cyprus -
Greeks in Southern Italy.
PRINTS & DRAWINGS
ORIENTAL COLLECTIONS
Japanese Galleries.

Monday-Wednesday, Saturday, Sunday 10.00-17.30, Thursday and Friday 10.00-20.30   *Free*
The Great Court is open late most evenings except Sunday for access to the restaurants etc.

MUSEUMS AND ART GALLERIES

APSLEY HOUSE, WELLINGTON MUSEUM G2 41

149 Piccadilly, W1. Built in 1778 by the Adam brothers: the Duke purchased the house from his brother after his famous victory at Waterloo. Until his death in 1852, a banquet was held in the house to commemorate his finest hour. Filled with pictures, porcelain, silver, plate and other relics of the Iron Duke. Probably the most singularly interesting item is the larger than life nude statue of his adversary Napoleon: one room of the house is decorated like a military tent of that era.
Tuesday - Sunday 11.00 - 17.00. *Charge*

BANK OF ENGLAND MUSEUM F3 37

Bartholomew Lane, EC2. Chronicling monetary history this museum resides within the walls of the great city bank. Models, bank notes, gold bars the complexities of exchanging money and dealing on the foreign exchanges will interest budding traders.
Monday - Friday 10.00 -17.00. *Free*

CLOCKMAKERS' MUSEUM E3 37

Guildhall, Aldermanbury, EC2. Attached to the Guildhall is this small museum. Watches, clocks and the chronometers used at sea to establish the position of longitude are here: includes John Harrison's H5.
Monday - Friday 9.30 - 17.00. *Free*

COURTAULD INSTITUTE GALLERIES G5 35

SOMERSET HOUSE, Strand, WC2. This is a superb collection of Impressionist and Post-Impressionist paintings and many other works bequeathed to the University of London. The finest of its kind in Britain, the collection includes works by Renoir, Degas, Manet, Monet, Seurat, Gauguin and Van Gogh, as well as Rubens and Van Dyck. *Charge. Daily 10.00-18.00 Free for under 18s, Mondays are Free 10.00 - 14.00 except Bank Holidays.*

DICKENS HOUSE MUSEUM G6 27

48 Doughty Street, WC1. From 1837-39, Dickens lived in this four-floored terraced house and wrote his novels *Oliver Twist* and *Nicholas Nickleby* during that period. His manuscripts, photographs, and lantern slides etc. are on view.
Monday - Saturday 10.00 - 17.00. *Charge*

DESIGN MUSEUM D6 52

Shad Thames, SE1 2YD. A rather austere building dedicated to 20-21st century design and focusing on everyday mass produced objects from motorbikes to household gadgets. *Daily 11.30 - 18.00.*

GUARDS MUSEUM C3 42

Wellington Barracks, Birdcage Walk, SW1. The Guards regiments were founded in the 17th century and their history is recalled with their weapons, uniforms, trophies and personal belongings.
Daily 10.00 - 16.00. *Charge*

HANDEL HOUSE MUSEUM H4 33

25 Brook Street, W1 Music and the interior decorations recreate the time from 1723-59 when the Royal Fireworks composer Georg Friedrich Händel once lived, worked and died in this house. *Tues, Weds, Fris, Sats, 10.00-18.00, Thurs 20.00 Suns 12.00-18.00 Charge*

HAYWARD GALLERY G1 43

South Bank, SE1. Adjoining the Queen Elizabeth Hall, the gallery is used for major art exhibitions. Always interesting displays, which is more than you can say for the exterior of the building.
Daily 10.00 - 18.00, Tues & Weds 20.00 Charge

IMPERIAL WAR MUSEUM A5 44

Lambeth Road, SE1.
Once part of a lunatic asylum called 'Bedlam', the museum illustrates the history of the two world wars and also more recent combat operations that involved Britain. You can experience what it was like in the trenches and in the East End of London during the Blitz. Large collections of photographs, paintings, decorations, weapons, uniforms, and full size aircraft suspended from the ceiling. *Daily 10.00-18.00 Free*

JEWISH MUSEUM H1 25

129-131 Albert Street, N1. Situated in Camden in a stylish extended townhouse you will find a collection of Jewish antiquities that illustrate both the private and the public religious life and history of the Jewish community in Britain. *Mons-Thurs 10.00-16.00.Closed Bank & Jewish Holidays. Charge*

LEIGHTON HOUSE C4 38

12 Holland Park Road, Kensington W14. Home of the celebrated Victorian artist Lord Leighton, who lived here until his death in 1896. Permanently on display are examples of High Victorian art with works by Leighton, Burne-Jones and Millais. The house is renowned for the beautiful Arab Hall, an authentic reconstruction of a Moorish palace banqueting hall. Fine period rooms of Victorian furniture, a collection of William de Morgan pottery and an attractive garden. Evening concerts.
Monday - Saturday 11.00 - 17.00. *Free*

LONDON CANAL MUSEUM F2 27

12-13 New Wharf Road, N1 9RT. The story of the canals and the people who lived on the narrow boats.
Tuesday - Sunday 10.00 - 16.30. *Charge*

LONDON TRANSPORT MUSEUM F4 35

Covent Garden WC2. In the flower market building of Covent Garden. This interesting museum illustrates the development of London's transport system with historic buses, trams, trolleybuses, and rail vehicles. *Daily 10.00 - 18.00* *Charge*

MUSEUM OF LONDON D2 36

Barbican, London Wall, EC2.
An intriguing display that defines the history, topography and rich heritage of London from prehistoric times to the present day.  Roman remains, models of the Roman forum and baths, Anglo-Saxon material, furniture, and clothing from Tudor and Stuart times, reconstructed shops and offices of Victorian and Edwardian days are just a few of the imaginative displays to be seen. Always attracting attention is the magnificent Lord Mayor's golden state coach and the Art-Deco elevator which used to whisk you to the restaurant at Selfridges. Look closely at the Map of Poverty on the walls and ceiling of a small alcove.
Tues-Sats 10.00-17.50, Suns 12.00-17.50. Open Bank Holidays Free

NATIONAL ARMY MUSEUM E3 49

Royal Hospital Rd, Chelsea, SW3. Imaginatively recording the story of British, Indian, and colonial land forces from Tudor times to the present day. Uniforms, weapons and personal relics of some great military leaders. Over 62,000 French, Prussian and English soldiers were killed at Waterloo in 1815. You can see a model of the battle and a film of it.
Daily 10.00 - 17.30 *Free*

NATIONAL GALLERY D6 34

Trafalgar Square, WC2. Situated in the domain of London's pigeons, the gallery holds an unequalled collection representing the European schools of painting and it is particularly rich in examples of Dutch and Italian works. There is also a large selection of British paintings from the works of Hogarth to Turner. Modern paintings are not on display here, for the cut-off year is 1900. Colourful works like Van Gogh's *Sunflowers*, the last Turner paintings and his *Fighting Temeraire*, Renoir's *Umbrellas*, and Seurat's *Bathers at Asnières* are all here. There are also some marvellous dreamy Claude Lorrain canvases, the classic *Haywain* by Constable and the *Rokeby Venus* by Velázquez.

Monday - Saturday 10.00 - 18.00, Wednesday 20.00, Sunday 12.00 - 18.00   *Free*

NATIONAL PORTRAIT GALLERY D5 34

St. Martin's Place, WC2. Interesting and often topical, this gallery tucked into the side of the National Gallery always holds your attention. Shakespeare to the Rolling Stones, that is the variety you get. Here are a few: all the Kings and Queens, John Donne, Cromwell, Nell Gwyn, the Brontë sisters, Lily Langtry, Byron, and Bernard Shaw. A couple of my favourites are Noel Coward, and the great Manchester United footballer Bobby Charlton

Mons-Sats 10.00-18.00, Suns 12.00-18.00. Free

NATURAL HISTORY MUSEUM A5 40

Cromwell Rd. South Kensington, SW7. Built in

1880 in the romanesque style, this fine, colourful terracotta building has zoological decorations along its wide facade. The departments incorporate Botany, Entomology, Minerology, Paleontology, Zoology and the Museum of Geology, renamed the 'Earth Galleries', and has some interesting features - an escalator ride through a portion of a rotating globe to the 'Power Within' exhibition which explains volcanos and simulates an earthquake. The film *Jurassic Park* stimulated interest in dinosaurs, and this museum has a moving, roaring, virtually real, almost frightening dinosaur! The new Darwin Centre building is a must-see expansion to the museum.....state-of-the-art science!

Mons-Sats 10.00 - 17.50, Suns 10.00 - 17.50. Free

QUEEN'S GALLERY. THE A3 42

Buckingham Palace Rd. SW1. Formerly the private chapel of Buckingham Palace, now used as an exhibition gallery, changing annually to display to the public a small part of the vast royal collection which includes famous artists' works, drawings, photographs and other works of art.   *Charge*

Opening Hours 09.30 - 17.30   Last Entrance 16.30
Entrance by Timed Tickets   ☎ 020 7766 7301

ROYAL ACADEMY OF ARTS B6 34

Burlington House, Piccadilly, W1. Founded in 1768 by Joshua Reynolds whose statue stands in the courtyard, the Academy is famous for its annual Summer Exhibition from May to September, which exhibits the works of living artists. Other exhibitions are also held throughout the year.

Daily 10.00 - 18.00   *Charge*

SCIENCE MUSEUM B4 40

Exhibition Rd. SW7. I always enjoyed my trips as a child to this museum; it was one of the first to allow you to interact in the discovery process. I have no doubt that children today find this museum one of the most interesting to visit. The museum traces many of the great achievements in the history and development of science and industry, and displays on five floors some of the original machines and equipment: steam engines like Stephenson's *Rocket* along with modern prototype locomotives. Mitchell's famous *Schneider Trophy Seaplane*, the forerunner of the Spitfire; the *Apollo 10* command module; veteran cars, and many other experiences that you can participate in: you can fly a plane, be an air traffic controller, mix and record music etc.

IMAX cinema book on ☎ *0870 870 4771   Charge*
Museum opens daily 10.00 - 18.00,   Free

SOANE MUSEUM G3 35

13 Lincoln's Inn Fields, WC2. Son of a bricklayer Sir John Soane (1753-1837) was an architect who was responsible for the windowless (for security) exterior wall of the Bank of England. His art collection and atmospheric house is filled like a magician's box with unforeseen revelations: Hogarth, Canaletto, Watteau, Reynolds, Turner and others are here along with Egyptian and Roman antiquities.

First Tuesday of the month 18.00 - 21.00,
Tuesday - Saturday 10.00 - 17.00.   Free

TATE BRITAIN E1 51

Millbank, SW1. Facing the Thames, this gallery contains British art from Tudor times onwards; the Turner collection is magnificent and includes his cerulean Venice paintings. You can view Hogarth, Constable, William Blake, the Pre-Raphaelites, Walter Sickert, etc., and sculptures by Henry Moore and Jacob Epstein. The restaurant is also notable, but it is unfortunately not open in the evenings.

Open Daily 10.00 - 17.50   *Free*

TATE MODERN C6 36

Bankside, SE1. Opened in 2000, the original Turbine Hall of the renovated Bankside power station makes an impressive introduction to this eclectic collection of international arts of the 20-21st centuries, includes works by Francis Bacon, Cézanne, Bonnard, Dali, Roy Lichtenstein, Magritte, Matisse, Mirò, Picasso etc., and sculptures by Rodin and Constantin Brancusi. On the top floor is a café which has fine views across London.   *Suns - Thurs 10.00 - 18.00,*
Fris - Sats 10.00 - 22.00.   *Free*

VICTORIA AND ALBERT MUSEUM B5 40

Cromwell Rd, South Kensington, SW7. One of the world's great and inspirational art collections with displays of fine and applied art of all countries, periods and styles. There are the great cartoons (tapestry patterns) executed by Raphael in 1516 for Pope Leo X, a large number of works by Constable, Tiffany glass, Limoges enamels, Post-Classical sculpture, Indian art, a Frank Lloyd Wright gallery, and at the rear of the museum the Morris and Gamble rooms, which are also worth seeking out. They used to be restaurant rooms.   *Mons 12.00 - 15.45,*
Tues - Suns 10.00 - 17.45, Weds 18.30 - 21.30. Free

WALLACE COLLECTION F3 33

Manchester Sq. W1. A superb collection of of art from all periods and from many lands especially France: pictures: Watteau's *La Toilette* - and 17th-18th century porcelain and furniture. There are also many examples of European and Oriental arms and armour, terracotta, jewellery, bronzes, and pictures by Flemish, Spanish and Italian masters. *The Laughing Cavalier* by Hals - the man that made lace come alive on canvas - is here!

Monday - Saturday 10.00 - 17.00,
Sunday 14.00 - 17.00.   *Free*

Sir Richard Wallace donated over 100 drinking fountains to the city of Paris

PLACES OF INTEREST

ALBERT MEMORIAL A3 40

Kensington Gore, SW7. This memorial was not of Albert's wish; nevertheless it is very impressive and is, if anything, a memorial to Victorian arts and crafts. The Prince Consort (1819-61) sits under a canopy holding the catalogue to the Great Exhibition of 1851, beneath him is a high relief frieze of 200 figures: musicians, poets, painters etc.

BANQUETING HOUSE E2 43

Whitehall, SW1. This was the only part of Whitehall Palace to survive the Great Fire. Designed in the Palladian style by Inigo Jones, it dates from 1619 and is noted for the fine allegorical ceiling paintings.

BRITISH LIBRARY, THE D4 26

96 Euston Rd. NW1. Not an attractive exterior but the brickwork does blend with the superb station adjacent. In the forecourt is an imposing bronze statue representing Sir Isaac Newton reducing the universe to mathematical dimensions, by Sir Eduardo Paolozzi. The library holds millions of books and manuscripts. It is a library of deposit: it receives a copy of every publication printed in Britain. Many works of art are on display throughout the library including in the entrance hall a marble statue of *Shakespeare* by Roubiliac dated 1758. There are three exhibition galleries where you will find treasures like the 7th century *Lindisfarne Gospels* (beautiful Celtic illuminated manuscripts), the *Magna Carta*, the *Gutenberg Bible* (the first printed book), and a 16th century Mercator Atlas. *Daily Mon-Sats 9.30-18.00, Tuesday 20.00, Sats 17.00. Suns 11.00-17.00 Free*

BENJAMIN FRANKLIN HOUSE E6 35

36 Craven St. WC2 Franklin - a scientist, an inventor, philosopher, and diplomat - was one of the most talented founders of the United States, he lived and worked here from 1757-75. The house built in 1730 in effect was the first US Embassy. *Weds-Suns 12.00-17.00 By Appointment* ☎ *(020) 7930 660* *Charge*

BRITISH AIRWAYS LONDON EYE G2 43

South Bank. This ferris wheel turns half-hourly. Climbing to 450 feet, the 33 capsules encompass wonderful atmospheric views over the river and London. Box Office County Hall ☎ *0870 5000 600 Daily 09.00-17.30. May-Sept 09.00-21.30 Charge*

BUCKINGHAM PALACE A3 42

The Mall, SW1. The London residence of the Queen the forecourt of which is guarded by the colourful sentries of the Guards Division, and the scene of the daily ceremony of The Changing of the Guard. *Daily May - August 11.30, weather permitting. Alternate days September - April.*
On August 7th 1993, the Queen for the first time opened the Palace State Apartments to the public. Designed by John Nash for George IV in 1826, the apartments contain beautiful brocades, furniture, clocks and paintings. The ticket office is in the Mall near the Victoria Memorial, on the Green Park side by Constitution Hill. Advance booking advisable. *Open from 7th August 9.30 - 17.30 approximately until the end of September.* *Charge*

CABINET WAR ROOMS D3 42

Clive Steps, King Charles St. SW1. The famous Map Room and the 21-roomed bunker and nerve centre used by Winston Churchill and his cabinet during World War Two: preserved with sound effects. *Daily April - August 9.30 - 18.00, September - March inclusive 10.00 - 18.00. Charge*

CHESHIRE CHEESE, YE OLDE B3 36

Wine Office Court, Fleet St. EC4. An ancient hostelry, rebuilt 1667, said to have been frequented by Dr. Johnson, Goldsmith and many other literary celebrities. Sawdust, uneven floors and a mention in Dicken's *Tale of Two Cities*.

CHURCHES OF INTEREST

ALL HALLOWS BY THE TOWER B4 52

Byward Street, EC3. A church was founded here in AD 675, but the present restored building dates from the 13th and 15th centuries. The church registers record the baptism of William Penn and the marriage of John Quincy Adams, later the sixth president of the United States. There are some good brasses in this church.

BROMPTON ORATORY C5 40

Brompton Road, SW7. The London oratory of St. Philip Neri. A Roman Catholic church with a wide nave built in the Baroque style in 1884, and noted for its music and choral recitals.

ST. BARTHOLOMEW THE GREAT C2 36

West Smithfield, EC1. An interesting and historic Norman building, once an Augustinian priory, and the second oldest church in London. Unfortunately the nave was a victim of the Dissolution and today it is nowhere near its original length. At one period, the Lady Chapel was used as a print shop where Benjamin Franklin came to work. The painter Hogarth, who lived nearby, was baptised here.

ST. HELEN'S, BISHOPSGATE H3 37

Great St.Helen's,, EC3. A survivor of the blitz, the Fire of London and an IRA bomb attack in 1993; this is one of the most pleasurable of the city churches.The 13th century nun's church has parallel naves, indicating that there were two churches - one was a benedictine nunnery. The church contains many monuments to city worthies, and is well known for its music.

ST. MARTIN-IN-THE-FIELDS E6 35

Trafalgar Square, WC2. Dating from 1726 this influential work by James Gibb has a temple portico and a 185 foot steeple; inside there is some very fine Italian plasterwork on the ceiling. Renowned for excellent free lunchtime concerts, winter candlelit concerts, brass rubbing and for the Café in the Crypt.

ST. PAUL'S, COVENT GARDEN E5 35

Covent Garden, WC2. Many parts of the Covent Garden area were owned by the Earl of Bedford: he commisioned Inigo Jones to build the Piazza and the church which dates from 1638, although it has been altered slightly when it was restored. Known as the 'Actors Church', there are many memorials to entertainment personalities: Charles Cochrane, Ivor Novello, Vivien Leigh, Noel Coward, Boris Karloff.

SOUTHWARK CATHEDRAL F6 37

Montague Close, SE1. A fine Gothic building that is second only to Westminster Abbey; the choir and chapel were built in 1207. Near the Shakespeare memorial is a stained-glass window depicting scenes from his plays. John Harvard, the founder of the American University, was baptised here in 1607: a chapel is dedicated to him. The new Chapter House contains a Pizza Express restaurant.

CLEOPATRA'S NEEDLE F6 35

Victoria Embankment, WC2. A pink granite obelisk 68 feet high, presented by the Egyptian viceroy in 1819, and floated here by sea in 1878. With a companion monolith in Central Park, New York, it stood at Heliopolis in 1500 BC.

DR. JOHNSON'S HOUSE   A3 36
17 Gough Square, EC4. The great man lived here from 1748 to 1759 where he wrote many of his works including his great Dictionary. *Mon-Sat 11.00 - 17.30 Charge*

ELEANOR CROSS   E6 35
Charing X Station, WC2. Many Gothic crosses were erected by Edward 1st where Queen Eleanor's coffin was set down on its route to Westminster. This Victorian replica stands east of the original location.

FLEET STREET   A4 36
EC4. Named after the old Fleet River, now a sewer running from Hampstead to Blackfriars into the Thames. It was "The Street of Ink." The newspapers have all gone now, but the street still has character.

GEORGE INN   F2 45
77 Borough High St. SE1. The surviving example of an old galleried inn well worth a visit. Famous as a coaching terminus in the 18th-19th centuries, it has a good restaurant with atmosphere.

GLOBE CENTRE   D6 36
New Globe Walk, Bankside, SE1. We have to thank American actor, Sam Wanamaker, for the persistence of his vision to rebuild the Globe near to the original site of the theatre where Shakespeare produced his

 plays. There is an exhibition, and during the summer the open-air theatre will demonstrate theatre as it was in Shakespeare's time. The restaurants have good river views and occasional music.
Daily May-September 9.00 -12.15, 14.00-16.00, October-April 10.00-17.00. Charge

GRAY'S INN   H1 35
Gray's Inn Rd. WC2. London has four great Inns of Court with the right to admit lawyers to practise as barristers in the English courts. They are Middle Temple, Inner Temple, Lincoln's Inn and Gray's Inn. *Monday - Friday 10.00-16.00. Gardens 12.00-14.00.*

GUILDHALL   E3 37
King Street, Cheapside, EC2. For more than 800 years the centre of civic government; the first mayor was elected in 1192. Begun in about 1411, only part of the walls, the Great Hall and crypt have survived. The Great Hall with monuments of famous people is used for the election of the Lord Mayor and Sheriffs. The eastern half of the 15th century crypt is notable for its six clustered pillars of blue Purbeck marble. A new building adjoining now houses: The Guildhall Art Gallery which displays works from the 16c to the present day: unearthed during building are the remains of a Roman amphitheatre. *Mon - Sats 10.00-17.00, Suns 12.00-17.00 Free* The Library has a unique collection of prints and books on the history of the city and also contains the Clockmakers Museum.
Open from 9.30 - 17.00 Monday - Saturday Free

HMS BELFAST   B5 52
Symons Wharf, Vine Lane, SE1. A famous World War Two cruiser permanently moored near Tower Bridge. Part of the Imperial War Museum the 11,500-ton cruiser played a leading role in European waters. *March-Oct. 10-18.00, Nov-Feb closes 16.00. Charge*

HORSE GUARDS   E1 43
Whitehall, SW1.
The Horse Guards building with its handsome clocktower was built in 1753. Here you see mounted sentries of the Household Cavalry: the Life Guards (scarlet tunics) and the Blues and Royals (blue tunics). The spectacle of the 'Changing of the Guard', takes place at 11.00 weekdays and 10.00 on Sundays. Approached through the archway is the extensive open drill ground Horse Guards Parade, which is the scene of the annual Trooping of the Colour ceremony before the Queen in early June.

HOUSES OF PARLIAMENT   E3 43
Palace of Westminster, SW1. The supreme legislature of the United Kingdom, a late-Gothic style building designed by Sir Charles Barry on the site of the former royal palace. The House of Lords, a lavishly decorated Gothic chamber, contains the throne of the Sovereign, the Woolsack, the seat of the Lord Chancellor and red leather benches for the peers. The House of Commons, rebuilt after war damage in its original style, has the Speakers chair and parallel rows of green leather benches for members. In the large Victoria Tower-336 feet to the top of the pinnacles - are stored many Parliamentary records. A part of the old 14th century Palace of Westminster to survive is Westminster Hall, which is renowned for its hammer-beam roof - it has been the scene of great historic events and trials.

Big Ben the Clock Tower, rising to 320 feet has four dials and houses the famous fourteen-ton bell which is struck hourly. When parliament is sitting there is a light above the clock. *Book well in advance to see Prime Minister's Question Time 15.00 - 15.30 on Wednesdays.* Debates on Mons - Tues - Thurs from 14.30, Weds & Fris 9.30, when in session. *In recesses 10.00-1700* ☎ 7219 4272

JEWEL TOWER   E4 43
Old Palace Yard, SW1. Another survival from the old Palace of Westminster built originally to house the King's private wealth and so used until the death of Henry VIII. Now a museum showing relics of the old palace and an exhibition of Parliament's history with a video. *Daily April - September 10.00 - 18.00, October - March 10.00 - 16.00 Tues - Suns. Charge*

KENSINGTON PALACE   F2 39
Kensington Palace Gdns. W8. A Jacobean building, the former residence of the Sovereign from 1689 to 1760 and later altered as the home of George 1. Many of the apartments are used for relatives of the royal family. The State Apartments include rooms by Wren and Kent, with portraits, furniture, the royal dress collection and mementoes of Queen Victoria and Queen Mary, both of whom were born in the palace. This was Princess Diana's last London residence - when they first married, Prince Charles lived here with her. *Daily 10.00 - 18.00 Charge Mid October - mid March Weds - Suns 10.00 - 16.00*

LAMBETH PALACE   G5 43
Lambeth Road, SE1. The official residence of the Archbishop of Canterbury for over 700 years. The famous Great Hall and other rooms contain many manuscripts and incunabula (early printed books). *Gardens open four times a year Saturday afternoons.*

LONDON AQUARIUM   G3 43
County Hall, SE1. A spectacular display of aquatic life, with fishes and invertebrates from all over the world, including sharks, sea scorpions, sting rays and deadly piranhas. *Daily 10.00 - 18.00. Charge*

LONDON BRASS RUBBING CENTRE   E6 35
St.Martins-in-the-Fields, Trafalger Square
Replicas of many fine church brasses are available here for visitors to make their own brass rubbing, with instructions and the materials supplied if required. *Charge Mons-Sats 10.00-18.00, Suns 12.00-18.00.*

MADAME TUSSAUDS & STARDOME   F1 33
Marylebone Rd., NW1. Renowned waxworks exhibition with figures of the famous and infamous from the past and present. The garden party, chamber of horrors and other striking tableaux.
Stardome the former Planetarium now explores earthly fame with a new visual experience hurtling you through space with a galaxy of stars!
Daily 9.00 - 17.30   *Charge*

MANSION HOUSE   F4 37
The Lord Mayor's official residence, renowned for the magnificent Egyptian Hall used for banquets. Underneath are prison cells where Emily Pankhurst, the suffragette, was once interned.

MARBLE ARCH   E4 33
A triumphal arch at the NE corner of Hyde Park. Designed by John Nash, it was originally sited in front of Buckingham Palace, but was removed to the present position when the palace was extended. The medieval Tyburn Gallows once stood nearby.

NELSON'S COLUMN   D6 34
Trafalgar Square.   Monument to Lord Nelson's victory at Trafalgar in 1805. A 167 foot high fluted Corinthian column made of granite by William Railton, topped by a 17 foot statue of the famous admiral. The bronze lions at the base were modelled by Sir Edwin Landseer.

OLD CURIOSITY SHOP   G3 35

Portsmouth Street, WC2.   In a turning off Kingsway, an antique and souvenir shop with a 16th century front, that claims to be the original *Old Curiosity Shop* made famous by Charles Dickens.

ROYAL COURTS OF JUSTICE   H4 35
Strand, WC2. The Law Courts in a huge Gothic building with over 30 courts and public galleries. The Central Hall is notable for its fine rose window.

ROYAL EXCHANGE   F4 37
Cornhill, EC3. Sir Thomas Gresham founded the Exchange in 1566. His crest, a grasshopper, is seen as the weathervane on the 180 foot high campanile. Every three hours from 9.00 - 18.00 tunes are played on a carillon. The exchange today houses boutiques, and is a very up-market shopping centre. *Free*
Monday - Friday 10.00 - 16.00, Sats 10.00 - 12.00

ROYAL HOSPITAL, CHELSEA   F3 49
Royal Hospital Rd., SW3. Founded in 1682 by Charles II for veteran and invalid soldiers. Originally designed by Wren with later building by Robert Adam and Sir John Soane. The "Chelsea Pensioners", of whom there are more than 500, wear traditional uniforms of scarlet frock coat in summer and dark blue in winter. The gardens are the scene of the annual Chelsea Flower Show.
Monday - Saturday 10.00 - 12.00, and 14.00 - 16.00.
Sunday 14.00 - 16.00   *Free*

ROYAL MEWS   A4 42
Buckingham Palace Road, SW1. Entered by an impressive Classical archway, the mews were built by John Nash, and house the Queen's unique collection of automobiles, coaches and carriages, as well as the coach horses. The main attraction is the fabulous Gold State coach which has been used for every Coronation since 1820.
Open from the end of March to the end of October except during state visits from 10.00 - 17.00
Ticket Sales ☎ *020 7766 7302*   *Charge*

SAATCHI GALLERY   E1 49
Duke of York's HQ, King's Road, SW3 4SQ
A contemporary art collection, often controversial, located in a long elegant Georgian building in Chelsea, which was previously used as a barracks.
Daily 10.00 - 18.00   *Free*

SHERLOCK HOLMES MUSEUM   E6 25
221b Baker Street, NW1. A small popular museum that makes the most out of Sir Arthur Conan Doyle's fictional character. On the ground floor is Hudson's Restaurant for tea!   *Daily 9.30 - 18.00*   *Charge*

SPEAKERS CORNER   E5 33
On the NE of Hyde Park near Marble Arch. Anyone can indulge in free speech without hindrance - other than hecklers - before a usually amused audience.

TEMPLE, THE   A4 36
Fleet Street, EC4. Of the four Inns of Court of the legal profession in London, two are here, Middle Temple and Inner Temple, in a quiet traffic-free oasis of lovely gardens and Georgian buildings. Here too is the Round Church, built by the Knight Templars in the 12th century on the model of the church of the Holy Sepulchre in Jerusalem, with a rectangular Early English chancel added a century later. Above the east gate is Prince Henry's Room built in 1610.

TOWER BRIDGE   C6 52
A unique drawbridge across the Thames - a symbol of London. The bridge's twin bascules, each weighing about 1000 tons, are between two huge Gothic towers, connected near the top by a fixed glazed walkway with panoramic views, and standing 140 feet above high water level. The central span measures 200 feet and the suspension chains on either side 270 feet. The bascules carrying the roadway are raised hydraulically to permit the passage of large vessels.
Museum daily April - October 10.00 - 18.30.
November - March 9.30 - 18.00   *Charge*

WELLINGTON ARCH   G2 41
Hyde Park Corner, W1. Triumphal arch built in 1825 by Decimus Burton topped by Adrian Jones's striking bronze quadriga, or four-horse chariot, which depicts *Peace Checking the Chariot of War*.
April - Sept 10.00-18.00, (Oct 17.00, Nov 16.00),
Wednesday - Sundays & Bank Hols.   *Charge*

WESLEY'S HOUSE & CHAPEL   F6 29
49 City Rd. EC1. This is an 18th century chapel and Georgian town house where the founder of Methodism lived. Mrs Thatcher got married here!
Mons - Sats 10.00 - 16.00, Sunday 11.00.

WESTMINSTER ABBEY   E4 43
Parliament Square, SW1. Subject to the Sovereign, not the church through a dean and chapter, the Abbey has been the crowning place of all the English monarchs since William the Conqueror: here too most of them since Henry III are buried. There are tombs and monuments to statesmen, warriors, poets and men of letters. Of interest is the Coronation  Chair, made for Edward I, and the Stone of Scone beneath, and upon which the Kings of Scotland and every English monarch since Edward I have been crowned. Poet's Corner in the South Transept is where to find the *Grave of the Unknown Warrior*. Once meeting place of the House of Commons, the Chapter House dates from 1250. The architect of the twin towers was Nicholas Hawksmoor, a pupil of Wren. They date from 1745.
Daily 8.00 - 18.00, Wednesday 20.00.   *Charge*

WESTMINSTER CATHEDRAL   B5 42
Ashley Place, SW1. The central Roman Catholic church in England. Seat of the Cardinal Archbishop of Westminster. A very large church constructed in 1903 in the Early Byzantine and the Romanesque styles with a pleasant piazza frontage. Built in alternate layers of red brick and portland stone it has a pleasing and unusual effect. The campanile, or tower is 273 feet high. *Daily 7.00-20.00.*
Charge to ascend the tower.

Christopher Wren was born in East Knoyle, Wiltshire in 1632. He went to Westminster School and then Oxford at the age of fourteen, where he studied mathematics and where later, at the age of 28, he became the Professor of Astronomy. In 1665, he spent six months in Paris studying architecture, the following year his opportunity came after the Fire of London had destroyed the city. He was asked to be the Surveyor-General and to prepare a master plan for the reconstruction of London. Unfortunately people began building very quickly and his plan for the whole city was not used: even today, the city is a haphazard muddle of buildings and alleys. We can only guess at the elegance and space his plan would have brought by marvelling at his great achievements: St Paul's and Greenwich Hospital in London, and the Sheldonian theatre in Oxford. These reach heights of dignity and classicism which have set the standards in English Architecture. Wren lived until 1723; he was 91 when he died, proof that work kills nobody.

MONUMENT, THE   **A4 52**

Fish Street Hill, EC3.   Wren built this 62 metre (202 feet) high fluted Doric column in portland stone between 1671-7, to commemorate the Great Fire of 1666, which broke out in Pudding Lane nearby. Some 311 steps lead up to a caged balcony - underneath a spiky ball - from which there are some great views of the city. *Charge Daily 9.30 - 17.30 Last admission 17.00*

ST PAUL'S CATHEDRAL   **D4 36**

 St Paul's Churchyard, EC4. Wren's majestic masterpiece, the largest and most famous church in London. The beautiful dome reaches to a height of 110 metres (365ft), and within the dome is the whispering gallery which has some quite amazing acoustic properties - try it out! Wren was 43 when the foundation stone was laid, and 79 when it was finished. The money to build the cathedral was raised by an importation tax on coal and wine coming in through London's docks. Wren's sojourn in Paris quite clearly helped him to formulate his inspiration and enthusiasm for classical and renaissance architecture. His first model of the cathedral - which when rejected they say brought him to tears - can be viewed in the crypt, where there are also numerous tombs of famous men including Wren and Nelson, Wellington, and Lawrence of Arabia. The dome ceiling was painted by James Thornhill who was nearly killed executing his work, which depicts the life of St Paul.

Many people will want to see *The Light of the World* by Holman Hunt, the Pre-Raphaelite painter; this you will find in the nave. In the south choir aisle is the only monument from the medieval St Paul's that survived the fire, the tomb of the Poet-Dean John Donne, "No man is an Island..." whose love poems live on to this day.

Only the young in heart and body should attempt the experience of climbing to the top; you can go just underneath the ball and cross, there are 628 steps for you to mount - count them!

Monday - Saturday 8.30 - 16.00.   *Charge*

There is no doubt at all that Christopher Wren was a great architect. However much doubt has been cast by hand-writing experts over the past few years as to whether he was responsible for so many of London's city churches. The fact that a Wren church equals a tourist attraction is probably responsible for the myths. As the surveyor-general, he must have been the overall supervisor, but as for the nitty-gritties, he would surely have delegated to those working in his office to get so much work done in such a short time. Here is a list of churches in chronological order:

ST MICHAEL, Cornhill. 1670-2.   **G4 37**
The nave is attributed to Wren.
ST VEDAST, Foster Lane. 1670-3.   **D3 36**
ST MARY AT HILL, St.Mary at Hill. 1670-6 **G5 37**
ST MARY-LE-BOW, Cheapside.1670-83   **E4 37**
Damaged by the luftwaffe, Bow Church - the original cockney church - was restored after the war; the original *Bow Bells* as the story goes, recalled Dick Whittington as Lord Mayor.
ST LAWRENCE, Gresham St. 1671-7   **E3 37**
ST BRIDE'S, Fleet Street. 1671-1703.   **B4 36**
When it was blitzed in 1941, Roman and Saxon remains were discovered; these can be viewed in the crypt. The telescopic steeple (68 metres or 226 feet) is Wren's tallest parish church steeple.It is said that it has been the blueprint for many wedding cakes!
ST MAGNUS, Lower Thames St.,1671-1705. **G5 37**
ST STEPHEN WALBROOK, 1672-1717.   **F4 37**
Many people regard this church as his finest - a mini St. Paul's. The Samaritans - who help people through their problems by listening - were founded here in 1953 by the rector Chad Varah: the poignant memorial to him is a telephone in a glass box. Another recent addition is the central white stone altar by Henry Moore.
ST JAMES, Garlick Hill. 1674-87.   **E5 37**
ST ANNE & ST AGNES,   **D3 36**
Gresham St.1677-80.
ST BENET, Upper Thames St. 1677-83.   **D5 36**
Said to be the work of Robert Hooke, a junior that worked in Wren's office, it somewhat resembles a Dutch church.
CHRIST CHURCH, Newgate St. 1677-87.   **C3 36**
The stylish tower is all that remains.
ST MARTIN, Ludgate Hill.1677-87.   **C4 36**
ST PETER, Cornhill. 1677-87   **G4 37**
ST CLEMENT DANES, Strand. 1680-2   **H4 35**
The Airforce church with a statue of the controversial Bomber Harris standing outside. James Gibbs, the architect of St.Martin-in-the-Fields and a great follower of Wren, finished the spire. He was also responsible for St.Mary-le-Strand (G4 35) which is now located on a traffic island.
ST MARY, Abchurch Lane.1681-6.   **F4 37**
A ceiling painted by James Thornhill.
ST MARY, Aldermary, Queen Victoria St. **E4 37**
1681-1704. Re-interpreted Gothic-style church.
ST JAMES, Piccadilly. (1682-84)   **B6 34**
A small parish church for Wren, not the site of a building damaged in the Great Fire. Bombed in WW2: now beautifully restored. Famous today for free lunchtime concerts and the daily craft market.
ST CLEMENT, Clements Lane. 1683-87   **F5 37**
ST MARGARET, Eastcheap 1684-89   **G5 37**
ST ANDREW, Queen Victoria St. 1685-95 **C4 36**
ST MARGARET, Lothbury. 1686-90   **F3 37**
ST MICHAEL, College Hill, 1686-94   **E5 37**
There were many other fine churches built by Wren that have now disappeared due to bombing in the Second World War. He lived on the south side of the Thames in Bankside opposite St.Paul's, in a house that still stands near the new Globe (D6 36).

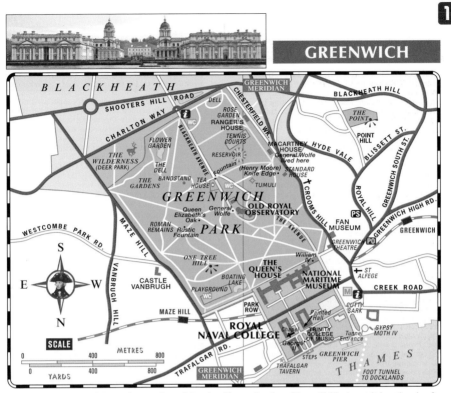

GREENWICH

Greenwich is a marvel. It so close to Central London (four miles from Tower Bridge), yet it has the air of a picturesque fishing village. Contrary, it also has probably the finest Classical - Baroque display of architecture in the country, by some of England's greatest architects: Inigo Jones, Christopher Wren, John Webb and Nicholas Hawksmoor. The best way to reach Greenwich is by river boat: there are cruises from Westminster, Charing Cross and Tower Piers. Alternatively, the Docklands Light Railway will take you to Island Gardens where you can walk across under the Thames (lifts take you down to the tunnel). The atmospheric view of the Naval College from Island Gardens is incomparable, particularly on a nice evening. On Saturdays and Sundays there is a very good Arts and Crafts market (see map) in the historic covered market.

ROYAL NAVAL COLLEGE Originally built as a Hospital for sailors between 1664-1702. The West river fronting building was by John Webb, and then Wren produced the plan we now see, incorporating the original building into the grand plan. **The Painted Hall** Arguably England's finest secular interior, designed by Nicholas Hawksmoor in the Baroque style, with marvellous paintings by James Thornhill, who painted the ceiling of St.Paul's. You can wheel a mirror trolley around to save craning your neck to view the painting - well worth seeing and it is free. It was here after Trafalgar that Nelson's body was brought to lie in state. **The Chapel** was designed by Wren and Ripley and completed after Wren died. It is interesting to note that the two busts on each side of the door are of 'Kiss me' Hardy, a friend of Nelson and the poet Keats. Hardy was also a 'Shipmate' of the Sailor King, William IV!   *Daily 14.30 - 16.45.*   *Free*

CUTTY SARK* In a dry dock and now a museum, this ship broke records ploughing her way to and from China with cargoes of tea and wool. *April-Sept. Mon-Sat 10.00-18.00, Suns 12.00-18.00, closed 17.00 Winter.   Charge*

GYPSY MOTH IV is the boat in which mapmaker, Francis Chichester, made the first round the world solo voyage in 1965-66.   *Small Charge*

THE NATIONAL MARITIME MUSEUM Very much devoted to Nelson and his historic achievements, there is a huge painting by Turner of the battle of Trafalgar. Of course that is not all: there are sections for Francis Drake, the practical Captain Cook and for John Franklin, whose name is recorded on maps of North America for posterity, reminding us of his relentless voyages to find the Northwest Passage.

The Queen's House A 17th century Palladian style villa by Inigo Jones that preceded everything else on the site. The wings were added after Trafalgar. The 'Tulip Staircase' is the star feature of the house.
Daily 10.00 - 17.00.   *Free*

ST. ALFEGE This is a church by Hawksmoor. Like a temple in concept. General Wolfe was buried here.

OLD ROYAL OBSERVATORY

Built by Christopher Wren, it now houses the Museum of Astronomy. To the left of the gates is the Meridian Building, which since 1884 has been the starting point of global measurement for time and space - the 'Prime Meridian'.The red *time-ball* rises every day at 13.00.   *Daily 10.00-17.00.   Free*

GREENWICH PARK Open from dawn until dusk, and originally laid out by Le Nôtre, of Versailles fame. The park is full of interest: a magnificent statue of General Wolfe at the top of the hill (a great place to take photos), Henry Moore sculpture, the remains of a Roman Temple, and a Deer Park are just a few of the features to look out for.

*Due to the fire and refurbishment the Cutty Sark reopens in spring 2012 - CHECK OPENING HOURS

London is world renowned for excellent and varied entertainments, especially music and theatre. For details the Saturday *Guardian* newspaper has a free supplement.There are also many free listing papers that you might find in your hotel lobby. *Time Out* publish a listing magazine, and there is always the *Big Issue* which helps the homeless.

Concert Halls

BARBICAN HALL   E1 37
Silk Street, EC2.   ☎ 7638 8891
This is the spiritual home of the London Symphony Orchestra. The hall also plays host to some of the leading orchestras in the world. Seating over 2000, with good sight lines and acoustics that have been improved over

ROYAL ALBERT HALL   A3 40
Kensington Gore, SW7.   ☎ 7589 8212
Built in 1871 as a memorial to the Prince Consort, this huge, beautiful amphitheatre with a dome of iron and glass can hold over 8000 within its circumference. The hall is not only used for classical music; there are all kinds of entertainment and sports held here. But it is the summertime Promenade Concerts which endears it to Londoners. The programmes of the *Proms* are always diverse and interesting (compared with the average concert). The last night is a memorable festive occasion. The organ is tremendous - I once remember nearly falling off my seat when the organ entered at the start of the Poulenc organ concerto!

CADOGAN HALL   F6 41
5 Sloane Terrace, SW1   ☎ 7730 4500
The building with a Byzantine style tower was formerly a church; now a concert venue, and the home of the Royal Philharmonic orchestra. Ecletic programming, good acoustics and a very intimate atmosphere are a feature.

ROYAL FESTIVAL HALL   G1 43
South Bank, SE1.   ☎ 7960 4242
Described by Aram Khachaturian as a large wheat granary when it was built for the Festival of Britain way back in 1951, this 2600 seat hall with its elm panels and excellent acoustics is still going strong after a major refurbishment. During intervals you can walk around the terrace and view the river.
Queen Elizabeth Hall Situated close by, with less than half the capacity of the Festival Hall, this is a more intimate venue suited for small orchestras or jazz orientated music.
Purcell Room Even smaller still; this is an ideal place to hear a piano recital or small jazz combo. The Queen Elizabeth and the Purcell Room are both comfortable venues, but the exteriors are very stark indeed which is unfortunate.

WIGMORE HALL   H3 33
Wigmore Street, W1.   ☎ 7935 2141
An elegant hall with plenty of marble and alabaster, forever linked with the piano manufacturer Bechstein who had the hall built to showcase his pianos (his shop was next door). It is a comfortable place for classical and jazz music, with very good acoustics.

ST.JOHN'S, SMITH SQUARE   E5 43
Smith Square, SW1.   ☎ 7222 1061
Used by the BBC for its lunchtime chamber concerts, this Baroque building is a popular venue for the office workers in the Westminster area.

Opera and Ballet

As a small boy my mother deposited me outside Sadlers Wells into the care of a school teacher friend for my initiation into Opera. I did not want to go and never said I enjoyed the experience. I did though, and I have loved Opera ever since. Opera today is very expensive and unfortunately a good seat for Covent Garden makes it a very special occasion. The English National Opera and Sadlers Wells are less expensive and they do have some very adventurous productions in very good theatres.

LONDON COLISEUM   E5 35
St.Martin's Lane, WC2.   ☎ 7632 8300
The flashing globe makes this 1904 Romansque style theatre instantly recognisable. Built by Oswald Stoll, it is very large (2350 seats) and is the home of the English National Opera. Opulent and inviting, this theatre is the place to see not only ENO but visiting opera and ballet companies. Lily Langtry and the famous Ballet Russe performed on this stage.

OPERA HOLLAND PARK   C3 38
Holland Park, W8.   ☎ 7602 7856
During the summer months you can see Opera and Ballet with a good standard of production performed under a large canopy in Holland Park. Previous productions include *Tosca* and *Eugene Onegin*.

ROYAL OPERA HOUSE   F4 35
Covent Garden, WC2.   ☎ 7304 4000
Preceeded by two other theatres, both destroyed by fire, this one dates from 1858 and is not only the home of the Royal Opera, but also the Royal Ballet. Situated in an attractive location it is now adjoined at the side to the small Linbury Studio Theatre and is much more accessible than it used to be. If you anticipate seeing a production I recommend the ballet, it is usually cheaper and the theatre is a lovely experience.

SADLER'S WELLS   B4 28
Rosebery Avenue, EC1   ☎ 7863 8000

Eclectic in its dance, opera and lyric programming, Sadler's Wells was never only accessible to the elite; the drawbacks were a small, sloping stage and a vestibule that was almost on the pavement. Now we have London's first new theatre of the 21st century; a great improvement, and a place to see the very best in international arts. Even the walls and ceiling surfaces can become an extension of the scenery and imagery on the stage.

Ticket Agencies

TKTS Booth   D5 34
Half Price Tickets with a small service charge are available for same day London West End productions from the booth situated on the south side of Leicester Square by the gardens. Open Monday to Saturday. *Matinees 12.00 - 14.00, Evening 14.00 - 18.30.*

KEITH PROWSE tickets   ☎ 0870 840 1111
24 Hour Credit Card Booking for London theatres, some cinemas, and South Bank Concerts etc. They also provide tickets for events throughout the world.

BRITAIN & LONDON VISITOR CENTRE   C6 34
Situated in Lower Regent's Street, tickets can be booked for West End shows.

TICKETMASTER   ☎ 0870 154 4040
Credit Card Booking for London shows, sports events, concerts etc.   24 Hour Booking.

Theatres

West End theatre is Shaftesbury Avenue; this is Theatreland. However, it spreads much wider now with the Barbican Centre and the South Bank contributing to the scene. London has only one rival in the world - Broadway. Here are a few theatres that I like and which might be of interest to you for their productions, architecture or decor.

ALMEIDA B1 28
Almeida Street, N1. ☎ 7359 4404
Situated in Islington, stars come here to act in its productions. Completely refurbished in 2003. Pinter plays have been premiered here.

AMBASSADORS D4 34
West Street, WC2. ☎ 7836 1171
Agatha Christie's *The Mousetrap* has played here since 1952 - what more can you say!

APOLLO VICTORIA A5 42
Wilton Road, SW1. ☎ 7630 6262
A large theatre and foyer built as a cinema in the 1930's. The theatre still retains its original almost subterranean decor, although the colouring which was blue and green has been altered.

BARBICAN E1 37
Barbican Centre, EC2. ☎ 7638 8891
The Royal Shakespeare Company live here as well as in Stratford. Although it has a large capacity all the seats are close to the stage. The Barbican Centre is also worth exploring.

HAYMARKET D6 34
Haymarket, SW1. ☎ 7930 8800
An 1831 theatre designed by John Nash. An ornate auditorium that saw the premieres of a number of Oscar Wilde plays.

HER MAJESTY'S D6 34
Haymarket, SW1. ☎ 7494 5400
Opened in 1897, the theatre had great success when it introduced Bernard Shaw's *Pygmalion*. In more recent times it staged the National's *Amadeus* and Andrew Lloyd Webber's *Phantom of the Opera*.

ROYAL NATIONAL THEATRE H6 35
South Bank, SE1. ☎ 7928 2252
Comprising of three theatres, the Olivier, Lyttelton and Cottesloe (in order of size). The buildings here with the Hayward Gallery always give me the feeling that Stalin will appear on the balcony. However the productions are excellent, and inside the buildings are spacious and comfortable.

OPEN AIR THEATRE F4 25
Regent's Park, Inner Circle, NW1. ☎ 7486 2431
One of the joys of summer are my annual visits to this theatre. Alfresco it is, so take an umbrella and something for a chilly evening. If you have never seen *A Midsummer Nights Dream* this is the perfect place - it is magical. Good buffet food underneath the amphitheatre and you can bring your own wine.

LONDON PALLADIUM B4 34
Argyll Street W1. ☎ 7494 5020
Designed as a music hall in 1910. The top names have all played here: Judy Garland, Danny Kaye, Frank Sinatra and Irving Berlin with his *This Is The Army* show. The ticket office wall is lined with posters demonstrating the fact that this was, and is, the mecca of light entertainment.

THEATRE ROYAL DRURY LANE F4 35
Catherine Street, SW1. ☎ 7494 5000
Two other theatres have stood on this site since the time of Charles II. This one dates from 1812 and is the largest theatre in London. Over the years many musical productions - *Oklahoma, Carousel, My Fair Lady, and Miss Saigon* - have been staged here.

Cinemas

Most of London's cinemas have lost their glamour The demand for choice has divided up the buildings so unless they were purpose built, the great decors appear to have gone. Here are some where you might care to see a good film.

CURZON MAYFAIR G1 41
Curzon Street, W1. ☎ 7369 1720
Real armchair comfort in the heart of Mayfair with programs featuring foreign and art films.

EMPIRE D5 34
Leicester Square, WC2. ☎ 0870 010 2030
Empire One is a good place to see a wide screen epic. My parents first date was in this cinema; if I tell you that the star was Lew Ayres, guess the film.

NATIONAL FILM THEATRE H1 43
South Bank, SE1. ☎ 7928 3232
Underneath Waterloo bridge, this is a repertory cinema, changing daily and showing great films and classics - Eisenstein through to Tarentino.

ODEON D5 34
Leicester Square WC2. ☎ 0870 505 0007
The largest ordinary screen and cinema in the metropolis. It is used for premieres, when celebrities bring panache to the occasions.

BFI LONDON IMAX H1 43
Waterloo Rd. SE1. ☎ 7902 1234
The largest screen in Great Britain, the place for a cinematic experience, rather than the latest film.

Jazz in London

Jazz in London is thriving. Some older clubs are still around, and thanks to the Pizza Express chain policy of providing jazz in their restaurants, venues have increased. *Ronnie Scott's* (D4 30) does not need an introduction: the perfect club, if only the clientele were real jazz fans. My memories apart from the late Ronnie Scott's jokes include standing next to Jane Russell in the vestibule: she had come to hear her friend, Anita O'Day (the lady with the hat in the film, *Jazz on a Summers Day*). Another extremely poignant memory was seeing Bill Evans two weeks before he died. From 12.00-16.00 on Sundays there is a Lunch Show.

The *Pizza Express* in Dean Street (C3 30) and in King's Road Chelsea at the Pheasantry (D2 44) both offer a menu of mainstream jazz and are highly recommended. The *100 Club* (C3 30) in Oxford Street has been going so long it is amazing. The traditional, blues, soul and dixieland music are accompanied here by a menu of simple food. Reasonable admission charges.

I like the *606 Club* (H6 43) in Chelsea; gourmet food, good modern jazz and it opens for seven days a week. The *Jazz Cafe* (D6 19) in a former bank building in Camden Town, offers the best in modern music and jazz and attracts some great musicians like Bobby Watson, José Feliciano. Often over the Christmas period, the place gently rocks to the music of the London Community Gospel Choir.

THE BULL'S HEAD On the southside of the river Thames near Barnes Bridge in Lonsdale Road, this pub has served jazz with excellent beer every day for many years. All the best musicians love the place; the audience is usually appreciative, and the music eclectic. Get a train from Waterloo to Barnes Bridge Station and walk about 30 yards, or go by the tube to Hammersmith and catch a 209 bus in the terminal to Barnes Bridge.

SERVICES AND USEFUL INFORMATION

Information Centres

BRITAIN & LONDON VISITOR CENTRE C6 34
1 Regent Street, Piccadilly Circus, SW1Y 4NS.
LONDON TOURIST BOARD
Telephone Information Service ☎ *0839 123 456*
Tourist Information Centres
Victoria Station, SW1.
8.00 - 19.00 Daily, Sunday 18.00.
Liverpool St. Underground Station, EC2M 7PN.
8.00-1800 Daily, Saturday & Sunday 8.30 - 18.00.
London Waterloo Station, SE1 7LT.
Daily 8.30 - 22.30.
City of London Information Centre
St.Paul's Churchyard, EC4   ☎ *020 7332 1456*
AIR TRAVEL
GATWICK *(flight enquiries)* ☎ *0870 000 2468*
HEATHROW   ☎ *0870 000 0123*
LUTON   ☎ *01582 405 100*
STANSTED   ☎ *0870 0000 303*
LONDON CITY   ☎ *020 7646 0000*
BRITISH AIRWAYS
156 Regent Street, SW1   ☎ *020 7434 4700*
BRITISH AIRWAYS CHECK IN TERMINAL at
Paddington Station, W2   ☎ *0845 779 9977*

WEATHER FORECAST   ☎ *0906 850 0401*

DOCKLANDS LIGHT RAILWAY
Docklands Travel Hotline   ☎ *020 7918 4000*
Travel Check   ☎ *020 7222 1200*

Emergency Services

AMBULANCE, FIRE, POLICE   ☎ *Dial 999*
MEDICAL SERVICE
University College Hospital
Gower Street, W1   [A&E]
St Thomas' Hospital
Westminster Bridge Road SE1
DENTAL SERVICE
Eastman Dental Hospital
256 Gray's Inn Road, WC1X
Mondays to Fridays 09.00 - 16.00.
Outside these hours go to a General Hospital.
EYE TREATMENT
Moorfields Eye Hospital
City Road, EC1
TRAFALGAR SQUARE POST OFFICE
William V Street, Trafalgar Square, WC2. [PO]
Mondays to Saturdays 08.00 - 20.00
LOST PROPERTY
For property lost in taxis or on the street apply to
any Police Station.
In taxis only, apply: 15 Penton Street, N1.
In Underground trains and buses apply
Lost Property Office: 200 Baker Street, NW1.
In Main Line Trains, contact the station master at
departure or destination stations.
In Department Stores, Hotels, Airports contact the
premises in question.
LATE OPENING CHEMISTS
Chemists in London districts work on a rotating
system for late opening. The lists are always
posted on the door or window. Otherwise the
local Police Station will have the information.

✁ **ELECTRICITY** ✁ 220/240 Volts with 3 pin plugs.
Shavers sockets have 2 thick round pins - do not use
     any other appliance in these sockets!

☎ *Prefix numbers with 020 when dialling
from outside CENTRAL LONDON*

AIRPORT TRANSFER
Heathrow The Piccadilly Underground Station
at Heathrow takes you into the centre of London.
The Heathrow Express runs every 15 minutes
from Paddington Station (full check-in facility for
20 airlines) taking 20 minutes. ☎ *0845 600 1515*
Airbus 2 Heathrow Shuttle (see Page 21): from
all terminals commencing at terminal 4 with four
departures an hour, 18 stops in Central London
finishing at Kings Cross Station.
Gatwick The Gatwick Express runs to and from
Victoria Station 04.30-06.00 and 20.00-00.30
every 30 minutes, from 06.00-20.00 it runs every
15 minutes. Allow approximately 35 minutes for
the journey   ☎ *0845 850 1530*
Stansted The Stansted Express operates to and
from Liverpool Street Station, the journey time is
approx. 40 minutes   ☎ *0845 850 0150*
An Airbus operates to and from the airport to
Victoria Coach Station.
BANKING HOURS
Banking hours are from 09.30-15.30 (although
many now stay open until 16.30) Mondays to
Fridays and with one exception all banks close on
Saturdays and Sundays. However some of the
larger department stores have banks and these
remain open during trading hours. Most banks
have cash machines outside available at all hours.
CREDIT CARDS
Most large shops, department stores, hotels and
restaurants will accept international credit cards
such as American Express, Diners' Club, Eurocard,
Mastercard and Visa etc.
PUBLIC HOLIDAYS
New Years Day January 1st
Good Friday (late March early April)
May Day (the first Monday)
Spring Bank Holiday last Monday in May
Summer Bank Holiday last Monday in August
Christmas Day December 25th
Boxing Day December 26th
INTERNATIONAL TELEPHONE CALLS
To make an international call dial 00 then dial the
Country Code followed by the individual number.
To make a call to London from outside the United
Kingdom dial the international code then 44.
TELEPHONE DIRECTORY ENQUIRIES
118 500 for numbers in the United Kingdom.
118 505 for International Numbers.
From a Public Call Box this service is free

CLOTHING and SHOE SIZES approximate						
SHIRTS						
Europe	36	37	38	39	40	41	42
UK and USA	14	14.5	15	15.5	16	16.5	17
DRESSES						
Europe	36	38	40	42	44	46	48
UK	8	10	12	14	16	18	20
USA	6	8	10	12	14	16	18
MEN'S SHOES						
Europe	39	40	41	42	43	44	45
UK and USA	6	7	7.5	8.5	9	10	11
WOMEN'S SHOES						
Europe	35.5	36	36.5	37	37.5	38	39
UK	3	3.5	4	4.5	5	5.5	6
USA	4.5	5	5.5	6	6.5	7	7.5

SHOPPING

People come from all over the world to shop in London and justifiably so, with two of the world's most celebrated department stores - Harrod's and Selfridges - and all kinds of shops and markets for any size of pocket. Off the map (Page 38 A2-3) is London's newest & largest shopping mall - Westfield.

Shopping Areas

BOND STREET A5 34
Divided in two sections - Old Bond Street and New Bond street. A street of fashionable shops and fine art dealers, with many respected names in fashion. Fenwick's department store, and home to Sotheby's the auctioneers.

BURLINGTON ARCADE B6 34
Running into Piccadilly and patrolled by uniformed beadles, it is very expensive but exquisite! Elegant specialist shops sell, silver, jewellery and knitwear.

CARNABY STREET B4 34
Associated with the Pop Culture and fashion of the 60s this colourful street became a legend. Today it still retains a unique atmosphere.

CHARING CROSS ROAD D3 34
A road that once never ceased to attract scholars and musicians. Although many antiquarian bookshops have gone, the unique Foyles in two buildings has survived. Music shops are on this street and in side turnings like Denmark Street.

JERMYN STREET B6 34
If you need shirts here is the place to have them made to measure. Expensive jewellery shops are here too with a perfumiers and a specialist cheesemonger.

KENSINGTON HIGH STREET D4 38
A popular shopping street for young fashions, boutiques and high-class couture, landmarked by the 1938 modernity of Barkers department store - now home to the Whole Foods Market.

KINGS ROAD, CHELSEA B3 48
Boutiques, pubs, bistros, antique dealers, and one department store on Sloane Square called Peter Jones (a John Lewis store). On summer Saturdays the road becomes one long art gallery where anyone can display their paintings.

KNIGHTSBRIDGE D3 40
Unequalled for its fashion, food and art shops. This is where to find Harrods and what was Lady Diana's favourite store, Harvey Nichols.

NEAL STREET E4 35
A relatively new thriving shopping area for young people close to Covent Garden piazza.

OXFORD STREET F4 33
London's most famous shopping street with large department stores including Selfridges, Marks & Spencer, D. H. Evans, and Debenhams etc. HMV has one shop for CDs and records. Just off the street near Selfridges is St Christopher's Place (G3 33) - a pleasant eating area.

REGENT STREET B4 34
This gently curving street of noble architecture is where to find the immutable yet changing department store Liberty's and the largest toy shop in Europe, Hamley's. Disney and Warner Brothers have also congregated alongside.

TOTTENHAM COURT ROAD C1 34
Apart from the great furnishing shop Heal's, this is the home of bargain HiFi; TV; Radio; Computers and almost anything electronic. Check around before you buy and you should get a good bargain!

> **TRADING TIMES*** *Shops usually open at 9.00 and close at 17.30 Monday to Saturday, closing at 19.00 on Thursdays in the West End, Wednesdays in Knightsbridge, Sloane Square and Kings Road.*

Department Stores

FORTNUM & MASON B6 34
Respected for its provisions department, tea, coffee, jams and aristocratic sales persona etc.

HARRODS D4 40
Above all else, do not miss the Edwardian food hall; it is out of this world, undeniably one of the world's greatest stores. See the fountain memorial to Princess Diana and Dodi Fayed on the lower ground floor.

HARVEY NICHOLS E3 41
Situated in Knightsbridge, stylish and well known for vogueish fashion with a very good food hall on the top floor.

JOHN LEWIS H3 33
The Oxford Street branch is the flagship of this standardised chain. Good quality products but not as interesting as some of the other stores here.

LIBERTY B4 34
Famous for its amazing 1924 Tudor-style building and its classic fabrics. Children will enjoy the clock outside - St.George chases the dragon every 15 mins.

SELFRIDGES F4 33
Spacious and renowned for its sales, the interior has recently been renovated. Above the main entrance is a superb Art-deco clock. Almost everything you need can be bought here. Delicious tea in the restaurants when you want to rest your feet.

Markets

BERWICK STREET C4 34
Soho's busy friendly fruit & vegetable market Monday to Saturday from 5.00 am.

BRICK LANE D1 52
London's curry centre, and heart of the leather industry, odds and ends etc. Sunday mornings.

BRIXTON Off the map area in an arcade and streets near the station. Worth a visit for the exotic sunny caribbean atmosphere - absolutely marvellous for fish. Monday to Saturday. Underground Brixton.

CAMDEN PASSAGE B2 28
Small Islington outdoor antique market, Weds & Sats.

CAMDEN MARKETS C5 23
A daily indoor market, arts, crafts, clothes etc. The outdoor market is a tourist attraction and is open from Thursday to Sunday.

CHURCH STREET B1 32
General market, good for antiques. Mons-Sats.

COVENT GARDEN F5 35
A covered market with buskers outside in the piazza to entertain you. Monday antiques, and Tuesday to Sunday arts and crafts 9.00 - 16.00.

LEADENHALL A3 52
Classic indoor market, incorporates the famous Lamb Tavern. Meat, poultry, fish, plants. Mons - Fris.

LEATHER LANE A1 36
Lunchtime market Monday to Friday.

NEW CALEDONIAN H4 45
Quality antiques, go early. Mons - Fris 6.00 - 14.00.

PETTICOAT LANE B1 52
Famous and large street market. Sundays am.

PORTOBELLO ROAD B3 30
Boutiques, antiques, almost anything. Mons - Sats.

OLD SPITALFIELDS C1 52
Antiques and crafts weekdays 9.00 - 17.00, Fridays and Sundays organic covered market.

**Sundays many shops in Central London open from approximately 11.00 to 17.30 especially in Oxford Street.*

LEGEND - ENGLISH - FRANÇAIS - DEUTSCH - NEDERLANDS - ITALIANO - ESPAÑOL

HOSPITALS
Hôpitaux
Krankenhäus
Ziekenhuisen
Ospedali
Hospitales

St.Mary's
Hospital

TOURIST INFORMATION
Informations Touristiques
Touristenauskünfte
Toeristen Informatie
Informazione Turistiche
Información Turística

i

POLICE STATION
Gendarmerie
Polizeiwache
Politie
Polizia
Comisaría

PS

FOOTPATH
Sentier
Fusspfad
Voetpad
Sentiero
Senda

POST OFFICE
Bureau de Poste
Postamt
Postkantoor
Ufficio Postale
Correos

PO

PUBLIC PARK
Jardin Public
Öffentliche Parkanlage
Publiek Park
Giardino Pubblico
Parque Publico

PHARMACY
Pharmacie
Apotheke
Apotheek
Farmacia
Farmácia

✚

CEMETERY
Cimetière
Friedhof
Begraafplaats
Cimiteri
Cementerio

HOTEL
Hôtel
Hotel
Hotel
Albergo
Hotel

DORCHESTER
■

RAILWAY STATION
Gares
Bahnhof
Station
Stazione
Estación

(EASTERN REGION)
**LIVERPOOL
STREET**

CHURCHES
Églises
Kirchen
Kerken
Chiese di
Iglesias

*St.
Helen's* †

OUTDOOR STATUES and SCULPTURES
Statues et Sculptures dehors
Im Freien stehende Standbilder und Skulpturen
Standbeelden en Beeldhouwkunst buiten
Statue e Sculture all'aperto
Estatuas y Escultura al aire libre

*Edith
Cavell*

SYNAGOGUE
Synagogue
Synagoge
Synagogen
Sinagoga
Sinagoga

✡

THEATRES and CONCERT HALLS
Théâtres et Salles de Concerts
Theater und Konzertsäle
Theaters en Concertzalen
Teatri e Sale dei Concerti
Teatros y Salas de Concertos

COLISEUM ■

JAZZ CLUB
Jazz Club
Jazz Club
Jazz Club
Jazz Club
Jazz Club

RONNIE
SCOTT'S ★

CINEMA
Cinéma
Kino
Bioscoop
Cinema
Cine

EMPIRE ■

DISCO or DANCE HALL
Disco ou Salle de Danse
Disko oder Tanzsaal
Disco of Dans Zaal
Disco o Sala di Danza
Disco o Salón de Baile

*The
Forum* ★

RESTAURANT OR CAFE
Restaurant ou Café
Restaurant oder Cafe
Restaurant of Café
Ristorante o Cafe
Restorant o Cafe

*Le Tour
de la Pont* ●

BUS ROUTE TERMINUS
Terminus d'Autobus
Endstation, Autobuslinie
Autobuslijn Eindpunt
Capolinea Autobus
Terminus de Linea Autobus

34

PUBLIC HOUSE
Pub
Ausschank
Herberg
Taverna
Taberna

*The
Spaniards ★
Inn*

TOILET Toilette Toilet Toeletta Retrete **WC**

BIKE STAND La Station Vélo Bike Station
Bicicletta stazione La estación de bicicletas ⊖

BARCLAYS CYCLE HIRE - for short
journeys Bike Stands are positioned
approx. 300 metres apart. The **Access Fee** is
£1 for a 24 hour period - return it inside
30 minutes and you will not pay the Usage
Charge............**be careful - you must wait
for at least 5 minutes between each trip!**
The **Usage Payment** or the Hiring
Payment is by Debit or Credit Card
online or at the docking station.

The **Usage Charge / 30 minutes are free:**

1 Hour...............£1	2½ Hours...........£10	24 Hours............£50.
1½ Hours..........£4	4 Hours...............£15	
2 Hours.............£6	6 Hours...............£35	

WHEN HIRING ALWAYS CHECK YOUR TYRES.
HIRING BEGINS WHEN THE KEY IS IN THE DOCKING POINT.
AT THE END OF A TRIP MAKE SURE WHEN YOU DOCK THE CYCLE - THE GREEN LIGHT GOES ON,
OTHERWISE YOU WILL CONTINUE BEING CHARGED!

CHECK THIS INTERNET SITE FOR YOUR NEAREST BARCLAYS CYCLE STAND AND READ
VERY CAREFULLY THE INSTRUCTIONS
http://www.//www.tfl.gov.uk/roadusers/cycling/14811.aspx

21

UNDERGROUND SYSTEM

MARBLE ARCH ⊖ The COLOURS of the Station Name Boxes indicate the Underground Lines that stop at the Station. *(Thus Marble Arch is on the Central Line)*

LE METRO LONDONIEN La COULEUR de la case portant le nom de la station indique la ligne qui la dessert. *(Example: la station Marble Arch est située sur la ligne Central)*

U-BAHN-NETZ Di FARBEN der Station - Namenschilder deuten auf die U-Bahn-Linien, die Stationen bedienen. *(Die Marble-Arch-Station liegt also auf der Central-Linie)*

METRONET De KLEUREN van de stationnamen geven de verschillende lijnen aan die op dat station stoppen. *(Dus Marble Arch Station ligt op de Central lijn)*

LA METROPOLITANA Il nome della stazione é dimostrato in COLORI rappresentativi delle differenti linee. *(Quindi la Stazione di Marble Arch si trova sulla linea Central)*

EL METRO La estaciones del Metro se indican en COLORES que representan las lineas. *(La Estación de Marble Arch está en la linea CENTRAL)*

UNDERGROUND LINE COLOURS

BAKERLOO   CENTRAL   CIRCLE   DISTRICT   NORTHERN   HAMMERSMITH & CITY

JUBILEE   VICTORIA   PICCADILLY   METROPOLITAN   WATERLOO & CITY   LONDON OVERGROUND

DLR   DOCKLANDS LIGHT RAILWAY   OVERGROUND RAILWAY

AIRBUSES - AÉROBUS - FLUGHAFENBUSVERBINDUNG - LUCHTBUS - AEROBUS - AEROBUS

AIRBUS A2 Heathrow Airport - Kings Cross Station

AIRBUS A6 Stansted Airport - Victoria Coach Station

A2 STOPS - Arrêt - Haltestellen - Stoppen - Fermata - Parada

STATION LINK SERVICE
Paddington • Marylebone • Warren St. • Euston • Kings Cross/St.Pancras • Islington • Old Street • Moorgate • Liverpool St. • Aldgate • Whitechapel Road • Whitechapel Station **205**

DAY BUS ROUTES WITH NUMBERS
Ligne d'autobus quotidienne avec numéros - Busstrecke tagsüber mit linien-nummern
Dagelijkse Autobuslijn met Nummers - Autobus quotidiano con Numeri
La Ruta de Autobuses durante día con Números

BUS ROUTES in GREY
Arrows indicate BUSES in one direction only.
Lignes d'autobus en GRIS. *Les flèches indiquent les lignes d'autobus dans un seul sens.*
GRAUE busstrecken.
Pfeile zeigen auf Busverkehr nur in Pfeil-richtung.
Autobuslijnen in GRIJS.
Pijlen geven de bussen aan in één richting.
Linee di Autobus in GRIGIO.
Le frecce indicano autobus in una sola direzione.
Ruta autobús en GRIS.
Las flechas indican la ruta de los autobuses en una sola dirección.

42 78

BUS ROUTE NUMBERS are indicated in the border.
Les lignes dépassant les bordures de la carte sont indiquées en marge.
Buslinien-Nummern sind am Kartenrand angegeben.
Bus route nummers zijn aangegeven in de kantlijn.
I numeri delle linee di autobus son indicate sul margine.
Los números de autobús se indican en el margen.

PLACES OF INTEREST - ENDROITS INTERESSANTS - SEHENSWÜRDIGKEITEN - BEZIENSWAARDIGHEDEN - LUOGHI DI INTERESSE - LUGARES DE INTERES

IMPORTANT BUILDINGS
Bâtiments importants
Wichtige Gebäude
Belangrijke gebouwen
Edifici importanti
Edifícios importantes

BANK OF ENGLAND

BUILDINGS open to the PUBLIC
Edifices ouverts au public
Allgemein zugängliche Gebäude
Gebouwen met toegang voor het publiek
Edifici aperti al pubblico
Edificios abiertos al público

ST.PAUL'S CATHEDRAL

SHOPPING - MAGASINS - EINKÄUFE - WINKELEN - ACQUISTI - COMPRAS

A SELECTION OF SHOPS - Choix de Magasins - Einige Läden - Keus van Winkels - Scelta di Negozi - Selección de Tiendas

LIBERTY

STREET MARKETS - Marché en plein air - Straßenmarkt - Straatmarkt Mercato all'aperto - Mercado callejero

M

TICKETS The TRAVEL CARD available for 1-3-7 days is the easy way to travel on the Tube, Buses, or Docklands Rail - it also gives 33% discount on River Services. The Central Zones 1-2 are probably all you will need: tickets can be obtained at Tube Stations or Tourist Offices. Note you can use a 1-2 zone ticket in all 6 zones on London Transport Buses.

KEY MAP

KILOMETRES
0   1   2   3
0   1   2
MILES

C

LONDON
CONGESTION
CHARGE ZONE

ALEXANDRA PALACE
NOEL PARK
WEST GREEN
TOTTENHAM HALE
WALTHAMSTOW
SOUTH WOODFORD
EPPING FOREST

HORNSEY
HARINGEY
RESERVOIRS

BRENT CROSS
EAST FINCHLEY
CROUCH END
FINSBURY PARK
STOKE NEWINGTON
STAMFORD HILL
SOUTH TOTTENHAM
HACKNEY MARSHES
LEYTONSTONE

GOLDERS GREEN
HIGHGATE
FINSBURY PARK
LEYTON

CRICKLEWOOD
HAMPSTEAD HEATH
56 **57**
HAMPSTEAD
SCALE 1:15,000
TUFNELL PARK
HIGHBURY
DALSTON
CLAPTON PARK
LEA VALLEY PARK

WEST HAMPSTEAD
GOSPEL OAK
KENTISH TOWN
HOLLOWAY

BELSIZE PARK
23

BRONDESBURY
SWISS COTTAGE
PRIMROSE HILL
CAMDEN TOWN
BARNSBURY
CANONBURY
HACKNEY
60
VICTORIA PARK
STRATFORD
OLYMPIC SITE
61 CITY
WEST HAM

KENSAL RISE
QUEEN'S PARK
KILBURN
ST JOHN'S WOOD
REGENT'S PARK
24 **25**
26
ISLINGTON
SHOREDITCH
SCALE 1:20,000
BOW
PLAISTOW

MAIDA VALE
27 **28** **29**
ST. PANCRAS
CLERKENWELL
BETHNAL GREEN

PADDINGTON
BLOOMSBURY
CITY
STEPNEY
BROMLEY

30 **31** **32** **33** **34** **35** **36** **37** **52**
NOTTING HILL
BAYSWATER
SOHO
TOWER
LIMEHOUSE

WESTFIELD SHOPPING MALL
MAYFAIR
WAPPING
CANARY WHARF
BLACKWALL TUNNEL
O2 ARENA

HYDE PARK
SOUTHWARK
ROTHERHITHE

HAMMERSMITH
38 **39** **40** **41** **42** **43** **44** **45**
HOLLAND PARK
BELGRAVIA
WESTMINSTER
LAMBETH
NEWINGTON
BERMONDSEY
MILLWALL

EARL'S COURT
CHELSEA
PIMLICO
WALWORTH
DEPTFORD

FULHAM
46 **47** **48** **49** **50** **51**
KENNINGTON
NEW CROSS
GREENWICH

WALHAM GREEN
BATTERSEA PARK
NINE ELMS
CAMBERWELL
GREENWICH PARK

BATTERSEA
PECKHAM
LEWISHAM

PUTNEY
CLAPHAM
BRIXTON
NUNHEAD
PECKHAM RYE COMMON
BROCKLEY
LADYWELL

WANDSWORTH
CLAPHAM COMMON
CLAPHAM PARK
BROCKWELL PARK
HERNE HILL
HONOR OAK

© MICHAEL GRAHAM PUBLICATIONS

SCALE

approximately 6 inches to 1 mile
1 CENTIMETRE TO 100 METRES

1:10,000

300 METRES EQUAL 328 YARDS

METRES
0   100   200   300

🏴 ENGLISH — The maps are divided into 300 metre squares with divisions of 100 metres indicated in the border.

🇫🇷 FRANÇAIS — Les cartes sont divisées en carrés de 300 mètres de côté, avec divisions de 100 mètres indiquées en bordure.

🇩🇪 DEUTSCH — Die karten sind in karrees von 300 quadratmeter unterteilt 100-Meter-Unterteilung ist am Rand markiert.

🇳🇱 NEDERLANDS — De kaarten zijn verdeeld in vierkanten van 300 meter met verdelingen van 100 meter in de kantlijn.

🇮🇹 ITALIANO — Le mappe sono suddivise in 300 metri quadrati con divisione di 100 metri indicate nel margine.

🇪🇸 ESPAÑOL — Las cartas están divididas en cuadrados de 300 metros, con divisiones de 100 metros indicados en el margen.

H
Oval Rd
Gloucester Cres.
Arlington St.
PARKWAY
Albert St.
DELANCEY ST.
St.

I

0
100
200
300

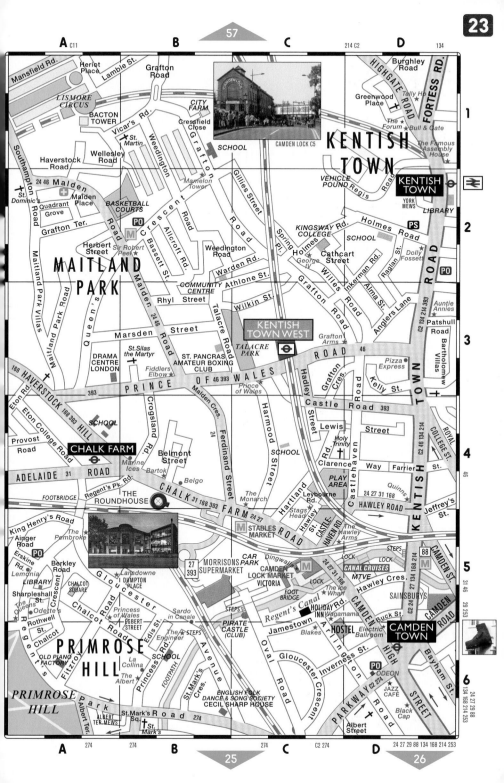

A C11   **B**   57   **C** 214 C2   **D** 134

CAMDEN LOCK C5

KENTISH TOWN

Mansfield Rd.
Heriot Place
Lamble St.
Grafton Road
Burghley Road
HIGHGATE ROAD
FORTESS RD.
Greenwood Place
Tally Ho
LISMORE CIRCUS
BACTON TOWER
Vicar's Rd.
CITY FARM
Cressfield Close
The Forum ★ Bull & Gate
Haverstock Road
St. Martin
Wellesley Road
Weedington
SCHOOL
Mamelon Tower
The Famous Assembly House

1

St. Dominic's
Malden
24 46
Southampton Road
Quadrant Grove
Malden Place
Grafton Ter.
BASKETBALL COURTS
Crescent Road
Gilles Street
VEHICLE POUND Regis
KENTISH TOWN
YORK MEWS
LIBRARY

2

Herbert Street
Sir Robert Peel ★
Bassett St.
Allcroft Rd.
Weedington Road
Warden Rd.
KINGSWAY Rd.
COLLEGE
Holmes Road
SCHOOL
Holmes
Spring Pl.
George IV ★
Cathcart Street
Willes Road
Inkerman Rd.
Alma St.
Raglan St.
Dolly Fossets
PO

MAITLAND PARK

Maitland Park Villas
Maitland Park Road
Queen's
24 46 Road
Marsden Street
Rhyl Street
COMMUNITY CENTRE
Athlone St.
Wilkin St.
Talacre Road
Grafton Road
Angler's Lane
Auntie Annie's
Patshull Road
Bartholomew Villas

3

HAVERSTOCK
168 393
HILL
Eton College Road
Provost Road
Adelaide Road
31
DRAMA CENTRE LONDON
St.Silas the Martyr
Fiddlers Elbow ★
ST. PANCRAS AMATEUR BOXING CLUB
393
PRINCE
Malden Cres.
OF 46 393 WALES
Prince of Wales ★
KENTISH TOWN WEST
TALACRE PARK
Grafton Arms
ROAD 46
Hadley St.
Grafton Cres.
Kelly St.
Pizza Express
Castle Road 393
Lewis Street
COLLEGE ST.
ROYAL
KENTISH TOWN ROAD
C2 134 214 393
C2 46 134 214
C2 214

4

Eton College Road
SCHOOL
CHALK FARM
Marine Ices
Bartok ★
Belgo ★
Crogsland Rd.
Belmont Street
Ferdinand Street
24
CHALK
The Monarch
SCHOOL
Holy Trinity ★
Hartland Road
Clarence Way
Farrier St.
PLAY AREA
Quinns
24 27 168
Hawley Road
Jeffrey's St.
46

5

King Henry's Road
Ainger Road
Erskine Rd.
Lemonia
LIBRARY
Sharpleshall St.
The Queens
Odette's ★
Rothwell St.
Chalcot
The Pembroke
Berkley Road
Gloucester
Lansdowne
DUMPTON PLACE
Chalcot Road
Regent's Pk. Rd.
FOOTBRIDGE
THE ROUNDHOUSE
27 393
MORRISONS SUPERMARKET
FARM ROAD
24 31 168 393
STABLES MARKET
M
CAR PARK
Dingwalls
CAMDEN LOCK MARKET
VICTORIA
Sardo in Canale
STEPS
Regent's Canal
LOCK
FOOT BRIDGE
The Ice Wharf
Hawley Cres.
24 27 31 168
MTVE
Stags Head ★
The Hawley Arms
88
STEPS
LOCK
LOCK
CANAL CRUISES
SAINSBURYS
M
CAMDEN ST.
CAMDEN ROAD
C2 134 168 214
27 134 168 214
31 46
29 253

6

PRIMROSE HILL
CHALCOT SQUARE
Princess of Wales ★
EGBERT STREET
Edis St.
The Engineer ★
STEPS
Sardo in Canale
PIRATE CASTLE (CLUB)
Jamestown Rd.
Blakes ★
HOLIDAY INN
Wagamama
HOSTEL
Electric Ballroom
CAMDEN TOWN
Buck St.
C2 214

Fitzroy
La Collina
The Albert
SCHOOL
Princess Rd.
St. Mark's Cres.
FOOTPATH
Avenue
Oval Road
Gloucester Crescent
Inverness St.
Arlington Road
PO
ODEON
JAZZ CAFE
Black Cap
HIGH
STREET
Bayham St.

PRIMROSE HILL
ALBERT Ter.
PRIMROSE Park
ALBERT TER. MEWS
St.Mark's Sq.
St. Mark's Road
274
St. Mark's ★
ENGLISH FOLK DANCE & SONG SOCIETY CECIL SHARP HOUSE
PARKWAY
C2 274
Albert Street
PO
24 27 29 88
134 168 214 253

A 274   274   **B** 25   274   **C** C2 274   **D** 24 27 29 88 134 168 214 253   26

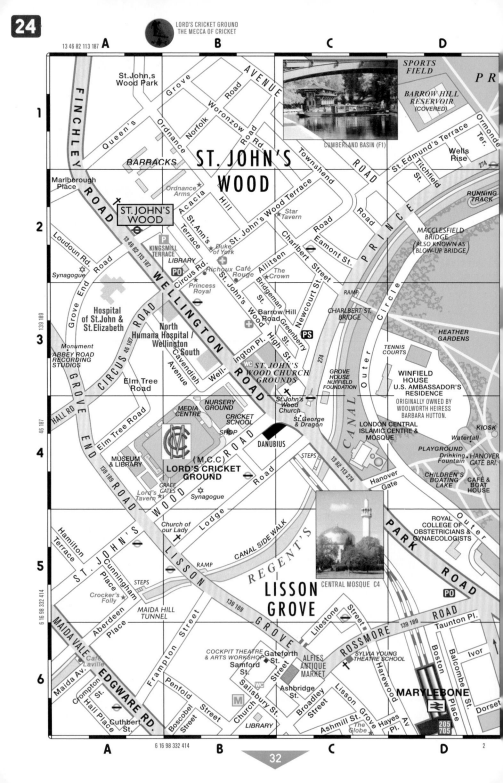

LIKE A PALACE JOHN NASH'S CUMBERLAND TERRACE (H3) IS THE MOST BEAUTIFUL OF ALL THE REGENT'S PARK TERRACES STRETCHING MORE THAN 250 METRES.

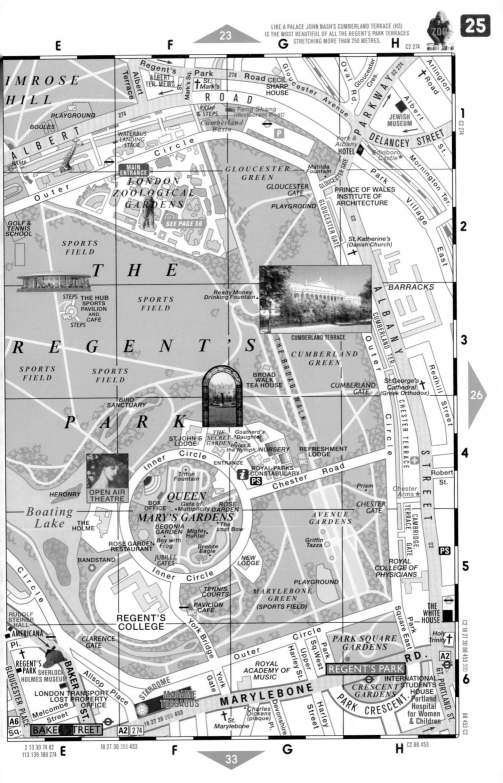

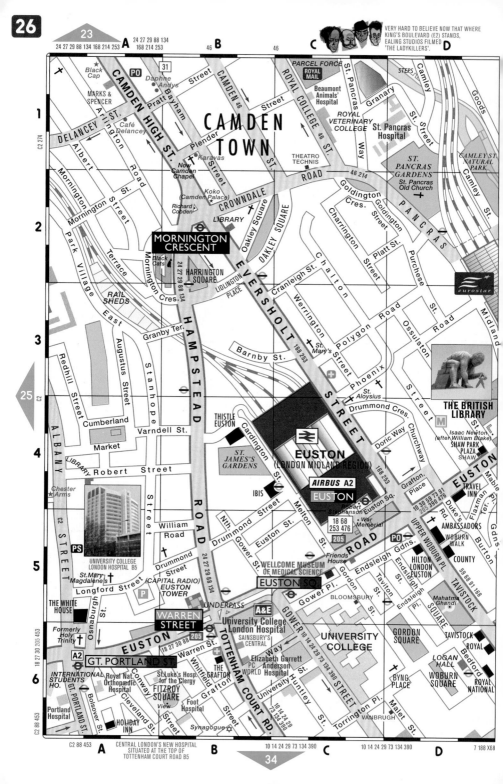

A 24 27 29 88 134
24 27 29 88 134 168 214 253   168 214 253

B   46

46   C

D

VERY HARD TO BELIEVE NOW THAT WHERE
KING'S BOULEVARD (E2) STANDS,
EALING STUDIOS FILMED
'THE LADYKILLERS'.

CAMDEN TOWN

Black Cap

PO

31

Daphne Antys

MARKS & SPENCER

Café Delancey

New Camden Chapel

Karavas

Koko (Camden Palace)

Richard Cobden

LIBRARY

CROWNDALE

MORNINGTON CRESCENT

Black Cats

HARRINGTON SQUARE

RAIL SHEDS

Granby Ter.

Barnby St.

Redhill Street

Cumberland Market

Varndell St.

LIBRARY

Robert Street

Chester Arms

UNIVERSITY COLLEGE LONDON HOSPITAL B5

St.Mary Magdalene's

William Road

Drummond Street

(CAPITAL RADIO) EUSTON TOWER

THE WHITE HOUSE

Formerly Holy Trinity

WARREN STREET

UNDERPASS

GT. PORTLAND ST.

INTERNATIONAL STUDENTS HO.

Royal Nat. Orthopaedic Hospital

FITZROY SQUARE

St.Luke's Hosp. for the Clergy

View

Foot Hospital

Portland Hospital

HOLIDAY INN

Synagogue

PARCEL FORCE
ROYAL MAIL

Beaumont Animals' Hospital

ROYAL VETERINARY COLLEGE

St. PANCRAS

ST. PANCRAS GARDENS

St. Pancras Old Church

Goldington Cres.

Goldington Street

Charrington Street

Platt St.

Purchese Street

Chalton

Cranleigh St.

Werrington Street

Polygon Road

St. Mary's Street

Phoenix Road

St. Aloysius

Drummond Cres.

Doric Way

Churchway

EUSTON (LONDON MIDLAND REGION)

AIRBUS A2

EUSTON

Robert Stephenson Euston Sq.

18 68 253 476

205

War Memorial

Friends House

EUSTON SQ.

THISTLE EUSTON

ST. JAMES'S GARDENS

Cardington St.

IBIS

Nth. Gower St.

Melton St.

Euston St.

Gordon St.

WELLCOME MUSEUM OF MEDICAL SCIENCE

PO

Endsleigh Gdns.

Gower Pl.

BLOOMSBURY

Endsleigh St.

Taviton St.

Endsleigh Pl.

Gordon St.

TAVISTOCK SQUARE

Mahatma Ghandi

UPPER WOBURN PL.

HILTON LONDON EUSTON

AMBASSADORS

WOBURN WALK

COUNTY

TRAVEL INN

SHAW PARK PLAZA

SHAW

Isaac Newton (after William Blake)

THE BRITISH LIBRARY

eurostar

CAMLEY ST. NATURAL PARK

Granary

STEPS

Camley

Goods

PANCRAS

Midland Road

Ossulston Street

A&E

University College London Hospital

SAINSBURY'S CENTRAL

Elizabeth Garrett Anderson Hospital

PC WORLD

UNIVERSITY COLLEGE

GORDON SQUARE

LOGAN HALL

BYNG PLACE

WOBURN SQUARE

VANBRUGH

Malet St.

Torrington Pl.

TAVISTOCK

ROYAL

LOGAN HALL

ROYAL NATIONAL

Bedford

EUSTON

WARREN STREET

Warren St.

THE GRAFTON

University Way

Huntley St.

Tottenham Court Rd.

Gower St.

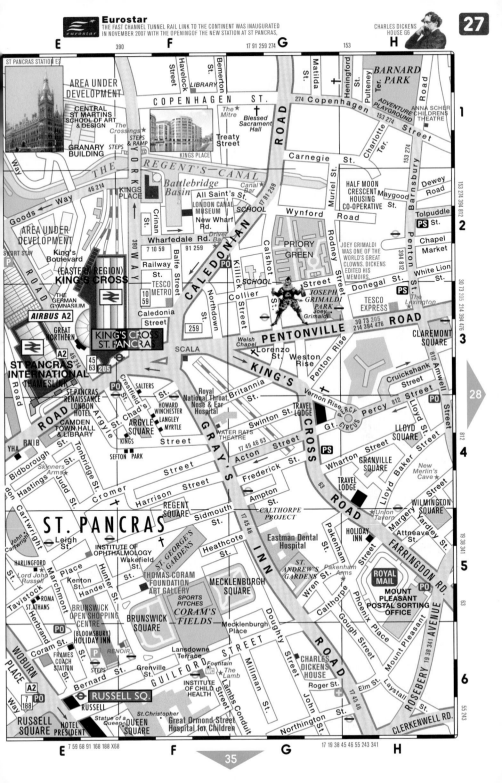

Eurostar
THE FAST CHANNEL TUNNEL RAIL LINK TO THE CONTINENT WAS INAUGURATED
IN NOVEMBER 2007 WITH THE OPENINGOF THE NEW STATION AT ST PANCRAS,

CHARLES DICKENS
HOUSE G6

27

E · 390 · F · 17 91 259 274 · G · 153 · H

ST PANCRAS STATION E2

AREA UNDER DEVELOPMENT

CENTRAL ST MARTINS SCHOOL OF ART & DESIGN

GRANARY BUILDING

The Crossings★
STEPS & RAMP
STEPS
STEPS

HAVELOCK Street
LIBRARY
BEMERTON St.

COPENHAGEN ST.

The Mitre★
Blessed Sacrament Hall
Treaty Street

KINGS PLACE

Matilda St.
Heningford
Pulteney Ter.
BARNARD PARK

274 Copenhagen Road

Carnegie St.
Charlotte Ter.

ANNA SCHER CHILDRENS THEATRE

ADVENTURE PLAYGROUND
153 274

153 274 394 812

THE REGENT'S CANAL

Battlebridge Basin

KINGS PLACE

Crinan St.

All Saint's St.
LONDON CANAL MUSEUM
New Wharf Rd.
SCHOOL
Canal Bar★
81 259

Wharfedale Rd.
Driver Bar
PO

Railway St.
Baffe Street
7 10 59
91 259

10 59
TESCO METRO

Caledonia Street
259

Wynford Road
Half Moon Crescent Housing Co-operative
PRIORY GREEN

JOEY GRIMALDI WAS ONE OF THE WORLD'S GREAT CLOWNS. DICKENS EDITED HIS MEMOIRS.

Muriel St.
Rodney Street
Donegal
Maygood St.
Penton
PS
Tolpuddle St.
Chapel Market
White Lion St.

PS
TESCO EXPRESS
The Laxington

30 73 205 214 394 812

153 274 394 812

AREA UNDER DEVELOPMENT

SHORT STAY
P

King's Boulevard
(EASTERN REGION)
KING'S CROSS

THE GERMAN GYMNASIUM

AIRBUS A2

GREAT NORTHERN

A2

ST PANCRAS INTERNATIONAL
THAMESLINK

KING'S CROSS ST. PANCRAS

SCALA

JOSEPH GRIMALDI PARK
Joey Grimaldi

PENTONVILLE ROAD

30 73 205 214 394 476

CLAREMONT SQUARE

ST PANCRAS RENAISSANCE LONDON HOTEL

CAMDEN TOWN HALL & LIBRARY

YHA RNIB

Crestfield St.
SALTERS St.

St. Chad's St.
Howard Winchester
Langley
Myrtle
KINGS
SEFTON PARK

ARGYLE SQUARE

Welsh Chapel
Lorenzo St. Weston Rise

Royal National Throat Nose & Ear Hospital

Britannia St.

WATER RATS THEATRE

Swinton St.
Acton Street
Frederick St.
Ampton St.

Penton Rise
Vernon Rise
Gt. PERCY CIRCUS
Percy

TRAVEL LODGE

Cruickshank Street
Amwell Street
812

Lloyd St.
PO

LLOYD SQUARE

New Merlin's Cave

Wharton Street
GRANVILLE SQUARE
TRAVEL LODGE

PS

Lloyd Baker Street

Yardley St.
WILMINGTON SQUARE
Attneave St.

Bidborough
Skinners Arms★
Judd St.
Tonbridge St.

Hastings
Cromer Street
Harrison Street

Sidmouth St.

CALTHORPE PROJECT

Eastman Dental Hospital

Pakenham Street
HOLIDAY INN

Margery
19 38 341

ST. PANCRAS

John Cartwright
HARLINGFORD
Lord John Russell★

Leigh St.
INSTITUTE OF OPHTHALMOLOGY
Wakefield St.
Hunter St.

ST GEORGE'S GARDENS

Heathcote St.

ST. ANDREW'S GARDENS

Pakenham Arms
Wren St.
Union Tavern
ROYAL MAIL

MOUNT PLEASANT POSTAL SORTING OFFICE
PO

Tavistock Place
ROMA
ST.ATHANS
Marchmont
Kenton
Handel St.
THOMAS CORAM FOUNDATION ART GALLERY

MECKLENBURGH SQUARE

Calthorpe St.
Phoenix Place
Gough Street

FARRINGDON RD.
63

HOTEL PRESIDENT

BRUNSWICK OPEN SHOPPING CENTRE
(BLOOMSBURY) HOLIDAY INN
PO
FRAMES COACH STATION
RENOIR
P
STEPS

BRUNSWICK SQUARE

SPORTS PITCHES
CORAM'S FIELDS
Mecklenburgh Place

Lansdowne Terrace
Grenville St.
Fountain
The Lamb★
WC

Doughty Street

CHARLES DICKENS HOUSE

Roger St.

Mount Pleasant
PO

ROSEBERY
19 38 341

WOBURN PLACE

A2
7 188
PO
Way

Coram St.
Bernard St.

RUSSELL SQ.

INSTITUTE OF CHILD HEALTH

GUILFORD STREET
Lambs Conduit St.
Millman St.
John St.

Northington St.

Elm St.
Laystall St.
CLERKENWELL RD.

55 743

RUSSELL SQUARE

Statue of a Queen
QUEEN SQUARE
St.Christopher
Great Ormond Street Hospital for Children

28

35

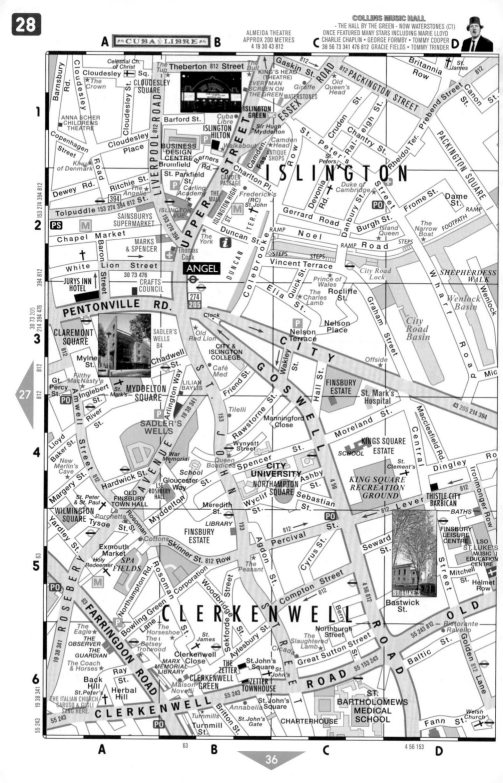

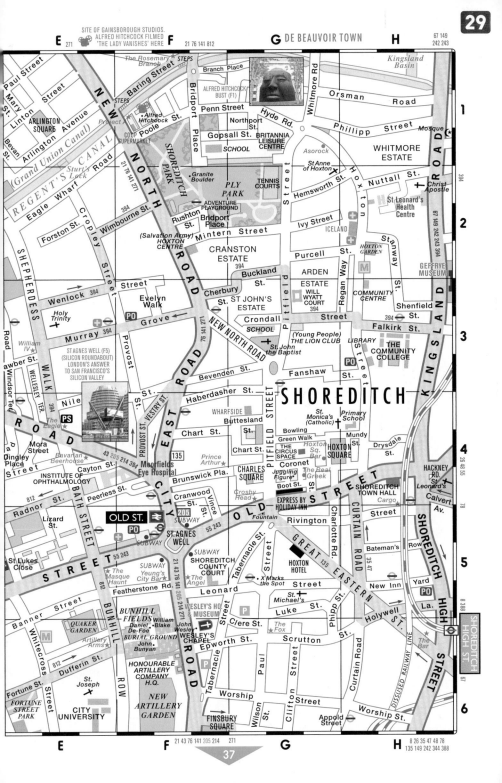

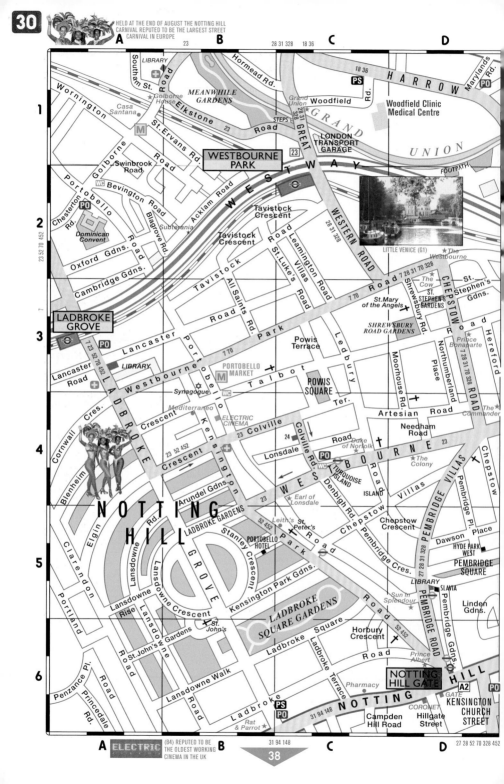

HELD AT THE END OF AUGUST THE NOTTING HILL CARNIVAL REPUTED TO BE THE LARGEST STREET CARNIVAL IN EUROPE

A   B   C   D

LIBRARY
Southam St.
Wornington Road
Golborne Road
MEANWHILE GARDENS
Hormead Rd.
Golborne House
Casa Santana
Elkstone Road
Grand Union
Woodfield
PS
HARROW
Marylands Rd.
PO
Woodfield Clinic Medical Centre

1

St. Ervans Rd.
M
Swinbrook Road
Portobello
Chesterton Rd.
PO
Dominican Convent
Bevington Road
WC
Blagrove Rd.
Subterania
STEPS
Great
Western Road
London Transport Garage
GRAND
UNION
FOOTPATH

2

Oxford Gdns.
Cambridge Gdns.
Portobello Road
Tavistock
Crescent
Tavistock
Crescent
All Saints Road
Acklam Road
St. Luke's Road
WEST WAY
Leamington Road Villas
23
WESTERN ROAD
St. Mary of the Angels
The Cow
St. STEPHEN'S GARDENS
St. Stephen's Gdns.
CHEPSTOW
Road
LITTLE VENICE (G1)
The Westbourne

WESTBOURNE PARK

3

LADBROKE GROVE
Lancaster Road
PO
LIBRARY
Westbourne Park Road
Portobello Road
PORTOBELLO MARKET
M
Synagogue
Mediterraneo
ELECTRIC CINEMA
Talbot Road
Powis Terrace
POWIS SQUARE
Ter.
Ledbury Road
SHREWSBURY ROAD GARDENS
Shrewsbury Rd.
Moorhouse Rd.
Northumberland Place
Prince Bonaparte
Hereford Road
The Commander

Lancaster Road

4

Cornwall Cres.
Blenheim Cres.
Elgin
Ladbroke Crescent
Kensington Park
Colville Road
24
Colville
Lonsdale Road
PO
WC
Denbigh Rd.
Duke of Norfolk
TURQUOISE ISLAND
ISLAND
Chepstow Villas
Artesian Road
Needham Road
The Colony
Chepstow Villas
Chepstow

NOTTING

5

HILL
Arundel Gdns.
Ladbroke Gardens
Stanley Crescent
Portobello Hotel
Leith's
St. Peter's
Earl of Lonsdale
WEST
Denbigh Rd.
Pembroke Cres.
Chepstow Crescent
PEMBRIDGE VILLAS
Dawson Place
HYDE PARK WEST
PEMBRIDGE SQUARE
LIBRARY
Sun in Splendour
SLAVIA
Pembridge Pl.
Pembridge Gdns.
Linden Gdns.

Clarendon
Portland
Lansdowne Rd.
Lansdowne Crescent
Lansdowne Rise
Kensington Park Gdns.
St. John's
St. John's Gardens
LADBROKE SQUARE GARDENS
Ladbroke Square
Horbury Crescent
Prince Albert
PEMBRIDGE ROAD
NOTTING HILL GATE
A2
PO

6

Penzance Pl.
Princedale Rd.
Lansdowne Walk
Ladbroke Terrace
PS
PO
Rat & Parrot
NOTTING
Campden Hill Road
Pharmacy
Hillgate Street
CORONET
GATE
KENSINGTON CHURCH STREET

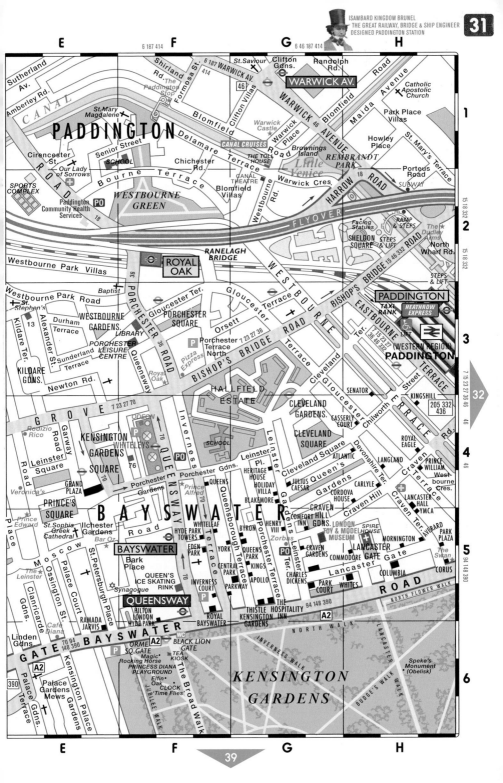

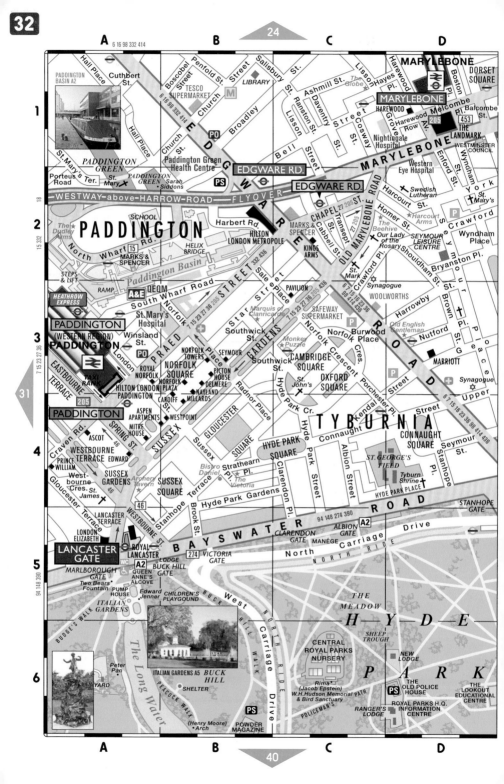

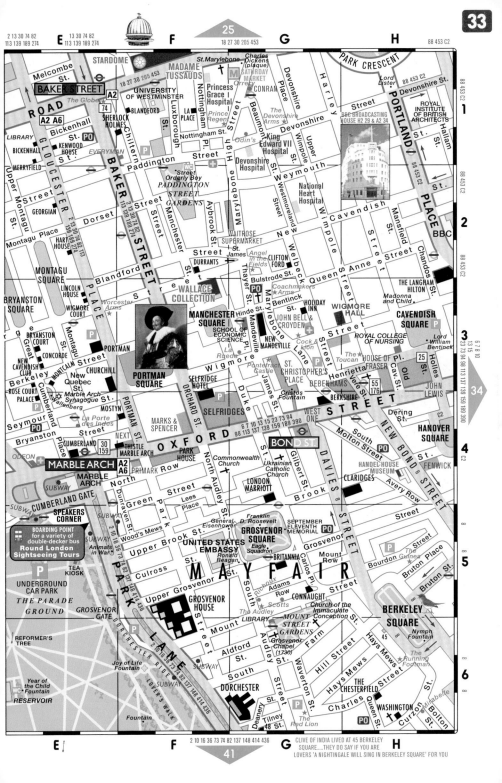

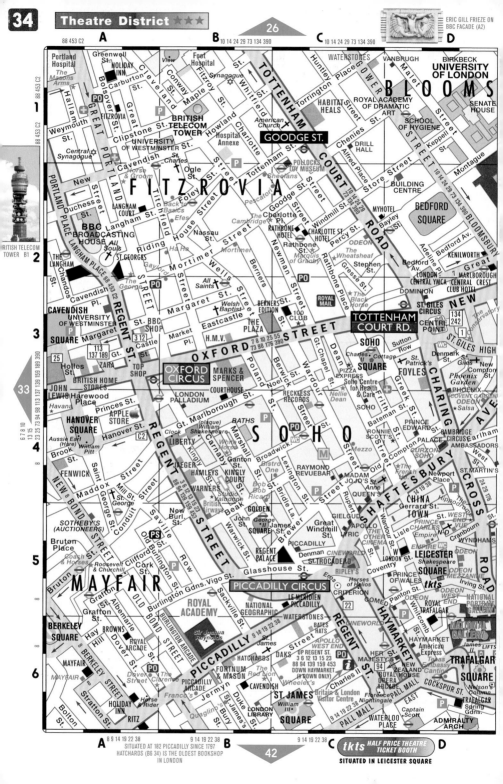

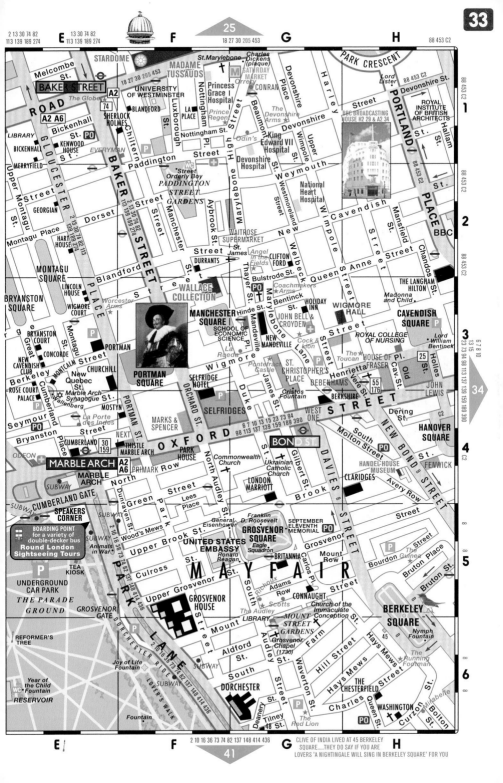

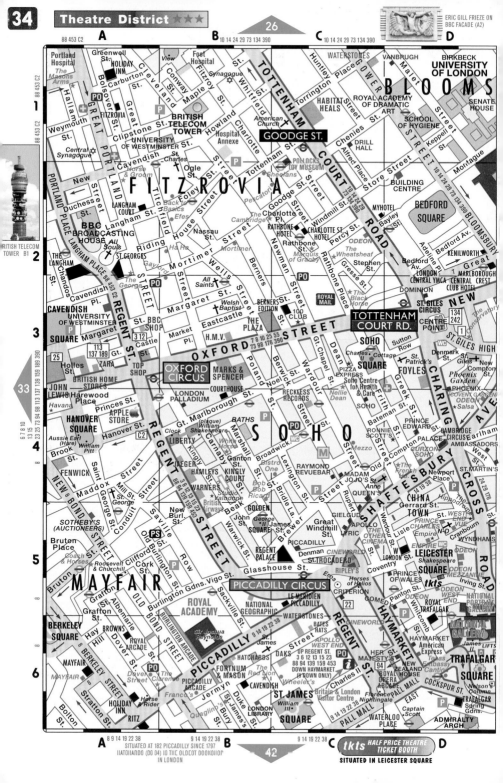

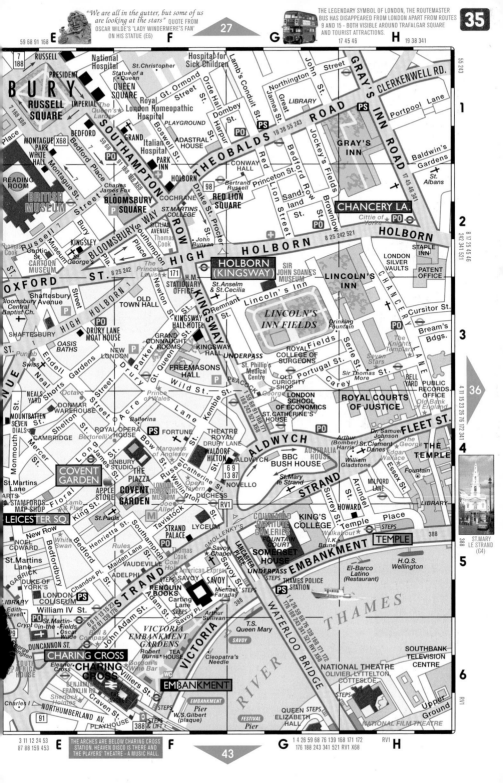

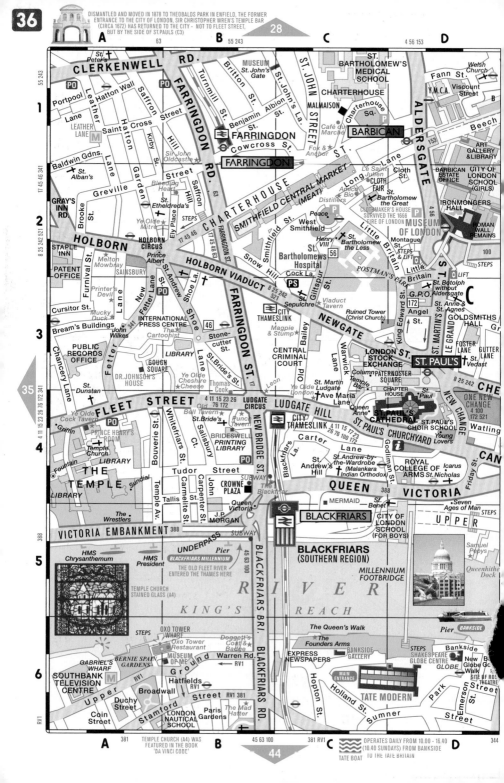

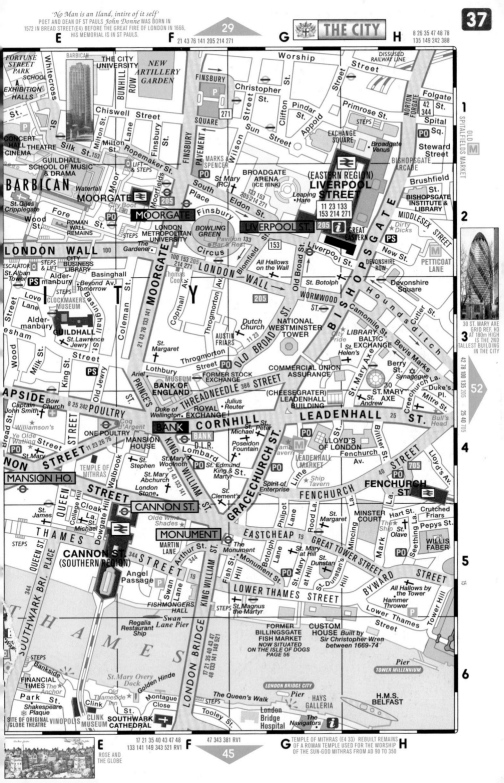

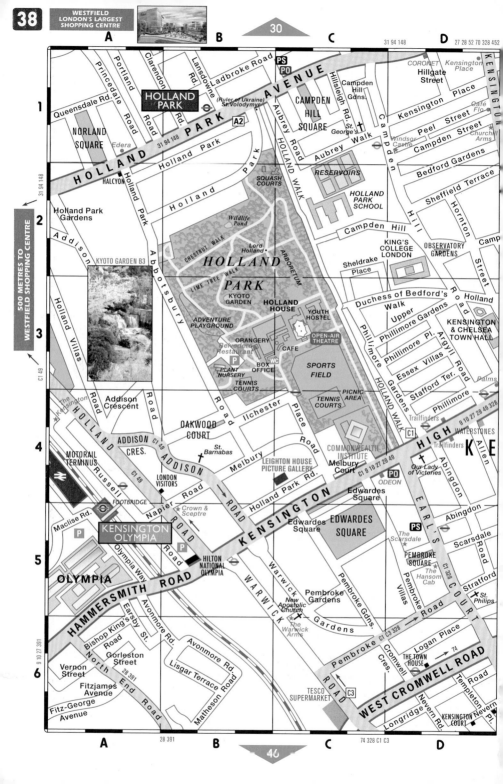

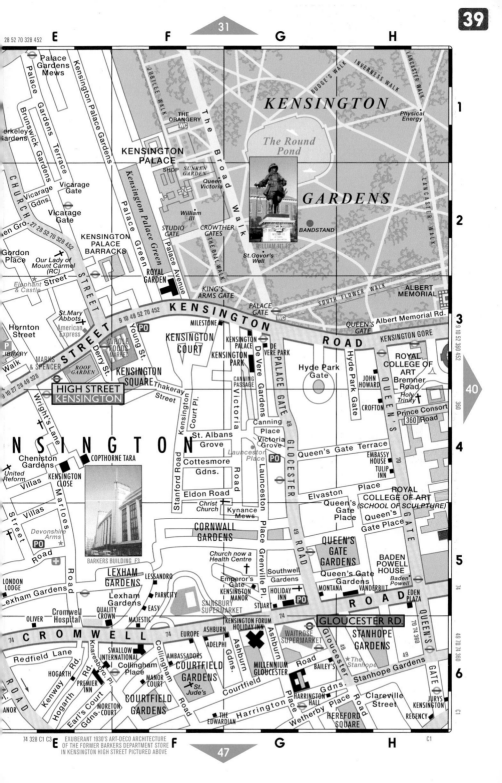

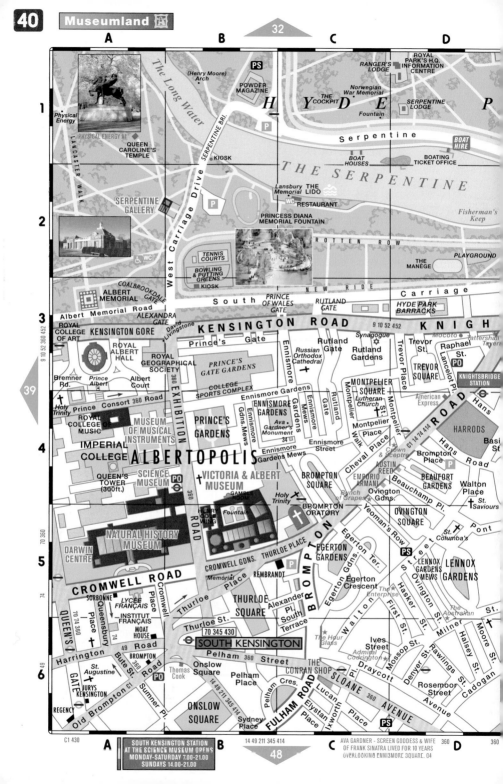

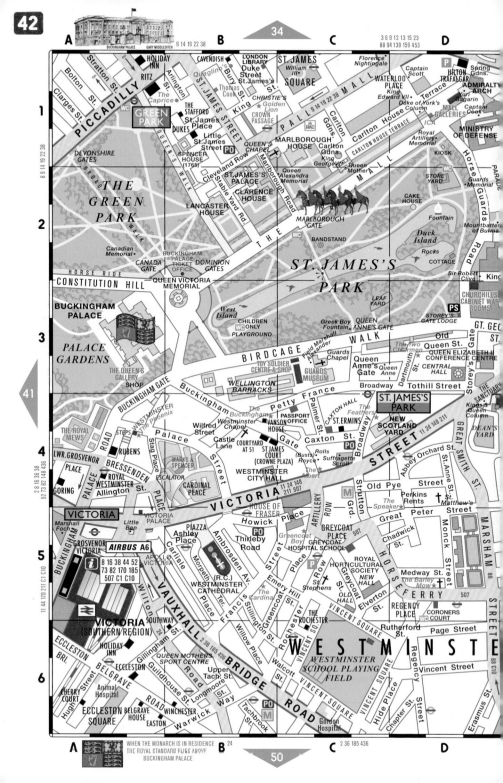

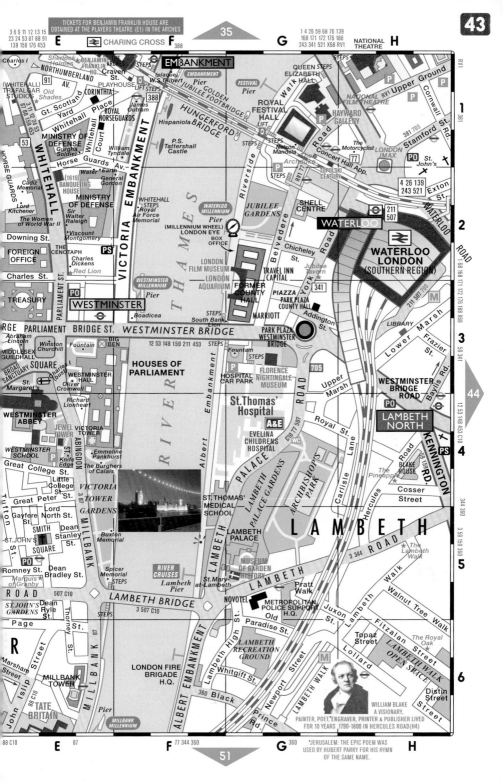

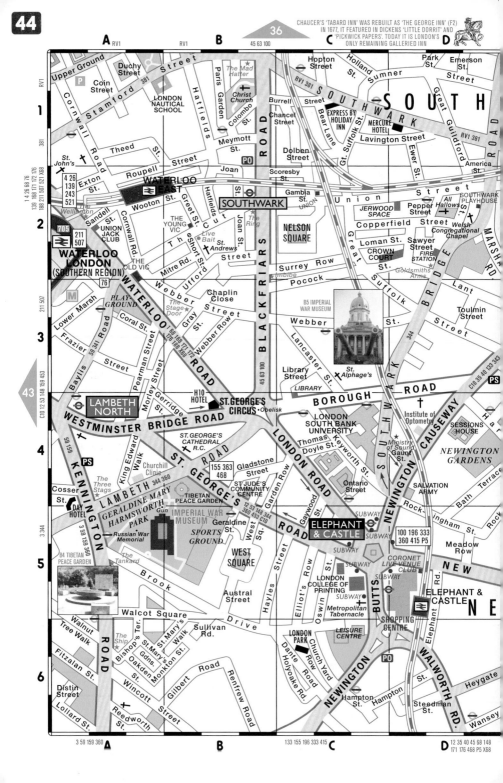

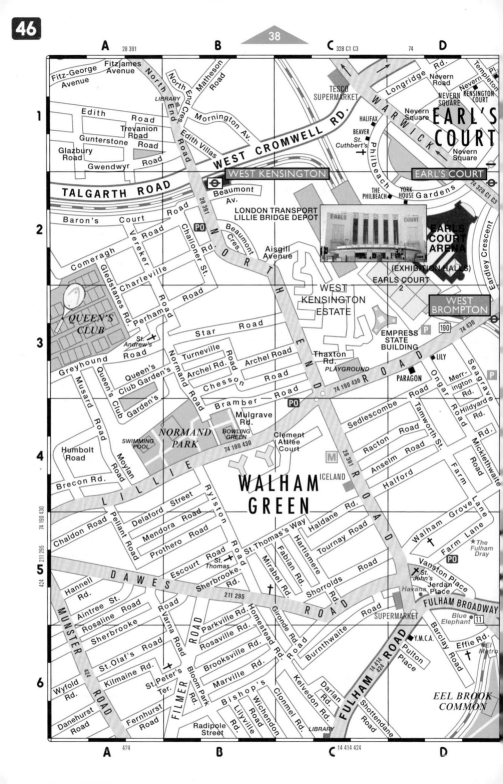

A 28 391 **B** 38 **C** 328 C1 C3 74 **D**

EARL'S COURT

Fitz-George Avenue
Fitzjames Avenue
North End Road
North End Cres.
Matheson Road
LIBRARY
Edith Road
Trevanion Road
Gunterstone Road
Mornington Av.
Edith Villas
Glazbury Road
Gwendwyr Road

Rd.
Longridge Rd.
Nevern Road
Templeton Pl.
Nevern Rd.
NEVERN SQUARE
KENSINGTON COURT
TESCO SUPERMARKET
WARWICK
HALIFAX
BEAVER St.
St. Cuthbert's
Philbeach
Nevern Square
Nevern Square

1

WEST CROMWELL RD.

TALGARTH ROAD

Beaumont Av.
WEST KENSINGTON
EARL'S COURT
THE PHILBEACH
YORK HOUSE Gardens
74 328 C1 C3

2

Baron's Court Road
Vereker Road
Challoner St.
Comeragh Road
Gledstanes Rd.
Charleville Road
Perham Road
LONDON TRANSPORT LILLIE BRIDGE DEPOT
Beaumont Cres.
Aisgill Avenue
NORTH END ROAD
WEST KENSINGTON ESTATE
EARLS COURT ARENA
(EXHIBITION HALLS)
EARLS COURT 2
Eardley Crescent
WEST BROMPTON

QUEEN'S CLUB
St. Andrew's
Star Road
Greyhound Road
Queen's Club Gardens
Turneville Road
Normand Road
Archel Rd.
Archel Road
Chesson Road
Musard Road
Queen's Club Garden's
Thaxton Rd.
PLAYGROUND
EMPRESS STATE BUILDING
74 190 430
LILY
Merrington Rd.
Seagrave Road
PARAGON
Ongar Road
Hildyard Rd.
Rd.

3

Bramber Road
Humbolt Road
Moylan Road
SWIMMING POOL
NORMAND PARK
Mulgrave Rd.
BOWLING GREEN
Clement Attlee Court
74 190 430
WALHAM GREEN
ICELAND
Sedlescombe Road
Tamworth St.
Racton Road
Anselm Road
Halford
Micklethwaite Road
Farm
Walham Grove
Farm Lane

4

Brecon Rd.
LILLIE
Chaldon Road
Pellant Road
Delaford Street
Mendora Road
Prothero Road
Ryiston Road
Escourt Road
St. Thomas's Way
Haldane Rd.
Hartismere
Fabian Rd.
Tournay Road
Road
ROAD
★The Fulham Dray
Vanston Place

5

Hannell Rd.
Aintree St.
Rosaline Road
Sherbrooke
DAWES
Sherbrooke Rd.
St. Thomas
Mirabel Rd.
Shorrolds Road
211 295
Road
SUPERMARKET
St. John's
Jerdan Place
Havana
FULHAM BROADWAY
Blue Elephant
11
El Metro

MUNSTER ROAD
Wyfold Rd.
Danehurst Road
St. Olaf's Rd.
Kilmaine Rd.
Fernhurst Road
St. Peter's Ter.
FILMER ROAD
Bloom Park
Varna Road
Road
Parkville Rd.
Rosaville Rd.
Brooksville Road
Marville Road
Bishop's Road
Homestead Rd.
Gironde Rd.
Wichendon Road
Lillyville Rd.
Clonmel Rd.
Radipole Street
Burnthwaite Road
Kelvedon Rd.
Darlan Rd.
Shottendane Road
FULHAM ROAD
Y.M.C.A.
Pulton Place
Barclay Road
Effie Rd.
LIBRARY
EEL BROOK COMMON

6

A 474 **B** **C** 14 414 424 **D**

74 328 C1 C3

E   F   G   H

CENTRAL LONDON'S CHELSEA FOOTBALL CLUB (E5)
OWNED BY RUSSIAN ROMAN ABRAMOVICH IS NOW ONE OF
THE WORLDS GREAT AND WEALTHIEST FOOTBALL CLUBS

47

39

C1 430

Kenway Rd.
MANOR
Hogarth Rd.
Earl's Court Gardens
COURTFIELD GARDENS
Collingham Gardens
THE EDWARDIAN
Harrington Gardens
Gloucester Road
JURYS KENSINGTON
Clareville St.
C1 430

K K HOTEL
GEORGE
PO
Earl's Court Rd.
BURNS
Courtfield Rd.
Collingham Pl.
Wetherby Gardens
HEREFORD SQUARE
REGENCY

LIVER
LAZA
Trebovir Rd.
BARKSTON GARDENS
Barkston Gdns.
Laverton Place
Wetherby Gdns
Gledhow Gardens
Bina Gardens
Rosary Gardens
CRANLEY
Brechin Pl.
ROYAL SOCIETY OF BRITISH SCULPTORS
ONSLOW GARDENS

HUNTERS LODGE
OXFORD
COMFORT INN
BARKSTON GARDENS
BRAMHAM GARDENS
COLLINGHAM GARDENS
C1 430

MOWBRAY COURT
Penywern Road
LONDON TOWN
Bolton Gardens
GLEDHOW GDNS.
C1 430
Drayton Arms
SWISS HOUSE
CRANLEY GARDENS
ROLAND GARDENS
CRANLEY GARDENS
Onslow Gdns

RASOOL
LORD COURT
JIM
Bolton Gardens
Y.H.A.
Y.W.C.A.
LIBRARY
Boltons Place
Cresswell Gardens
Drayton Gardens
BLAKES
Roland Gardens
EVELYN GARDENS

WEMBAR
EARL'S COURT SQUARE
EARL'S COURT SQUARE
Langans
Balans West
COLEHERNE COURT
St. Luke's
The Boltons
St Mary the Boltons
Cresswell Place
Priory Walk
Evelyn Gardens
THISTLE GROVE

NORTH LODGE
Charles Collins (Painter)
Richard Tauber
REDCLIFFE SQUARE
Coleherne Rd.
Westgate Ter.
Harcourt Terrace
The Little Boltons
Tregunter Road
Harley Gardens
Gilston Road
Milborne Grove
CINEWORLD
BEAUFORT ST.

Emmeline Pankhurst
John Wisden (Cricketer)
(Mountain Fame) Sir George Everest
REDCLIFFE SQUARE
WEST BROMPTON
Redcliffe St.
Cathcart Rd.
Hollywood Road
The Hollywood
Redcliffe Road
Goat In Boots
Callow St.
Elm Park Rd.
345

Brigade of Guards Monument
Frederic Leyland (Painter)
Val Prinsep
(Boxer) Gentleman John Jackson
Samuel Cunard (Shipping Magnet)
Finborough Arms
Finborough Road
Ifield Road
328 C3
328 C3
Glaister's Garden
Pizza Express
Limerston St.
Camera Place
Park Walk
The Sporting Page

SEE TOMB OF FREDERICK LEYLAND (ARTS & CRAFTS)
BROMPTON CEMETERY
Down the field
Fawcett Road
St. Mary's
PO
Chelsea and Westminster Hospital
A&E

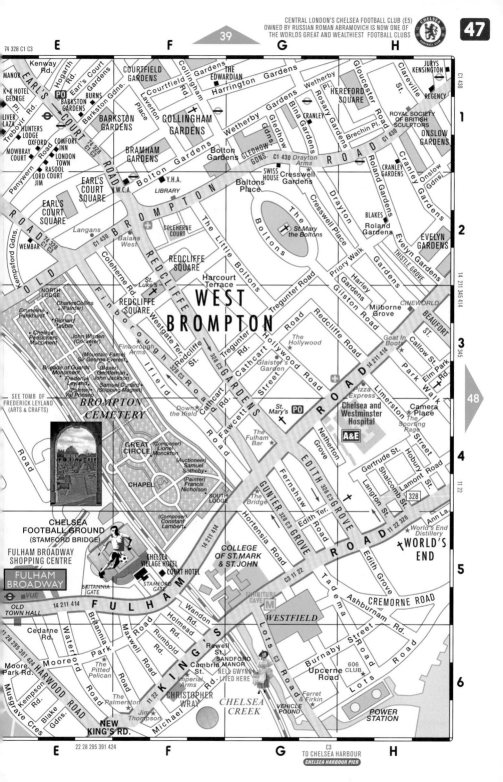

GREAT CIRCLE
(Composer) Lionel Monckton
(Auctioneer) Samuel Sotheby
St. Mary's
The Fulham Bar
Netherton Grove
Gertrude St.
Hobury St.
Shalcomb St.
Lamont Road

CHAPEL
(Painter) Francis Nicholson
SOUTH LODGE
The Bridge
EDITH GROVE
Fernshaw Road
Langton St.
328

CHELSEA FOOTBALL GROUND (STAMFORD BRIDGE)
(Composer) Constant Lambert
Hortensia Road
Edith Ter.
World's End Distillery

FULHAM BROADWAY SHOPPING CENTRE
FULHAM BROADWAY
BRITANNIA GATE
CHELSEA VILLAGE HOTEL
STAMFORD COURT HOTEL
COLLEGE OF ST. MARK & ST. JOHN
GUNTER GROVE
EDITH GROVE
Ann La.
WORLD'S END

OLD TOWN HALL
VUE
14 211 414
FULHAM ROAD
Wandon Rd.
Holmead Rd.
WESTFIELD
Tadema Road
Ashburnham Rd.
CREMORNE ROAD

Cedarne Rd.
Moore Park Rd.
MOOREHOUSE
HARWOOD ROAD
Waterford Rd.
BRITANNIA
Park
Maxwell Road
Rumbold Rd.
Rewell St.
SANDFORD St.
Cambria St.
Lots Road
Upcerne Road
606 CLUB
Burnaby Street
Lots Road

Musgrave Cres.
Kempson Rd.
Blake Gdns.
The Pitted Pelican
KING'S ROAD
The Palmerston
Jim Thompson
CHRISTOPHER WRAY
Michael Rd.
NELL GWYNN LIVED HERE
Imperial Arms
MANOR
CHELSEA CREEK
VEHICLE POUND
Ferret & Firkin
POWER STATION

NEW KING'S RD.

C1 430
14 211 345 414
345
48
11 22

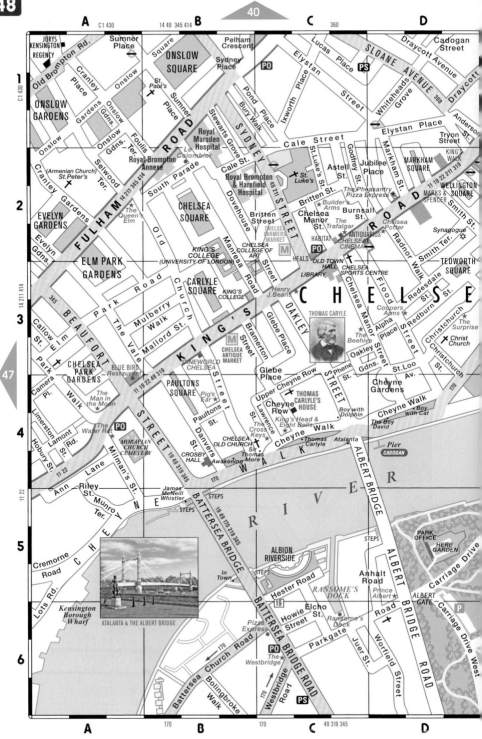

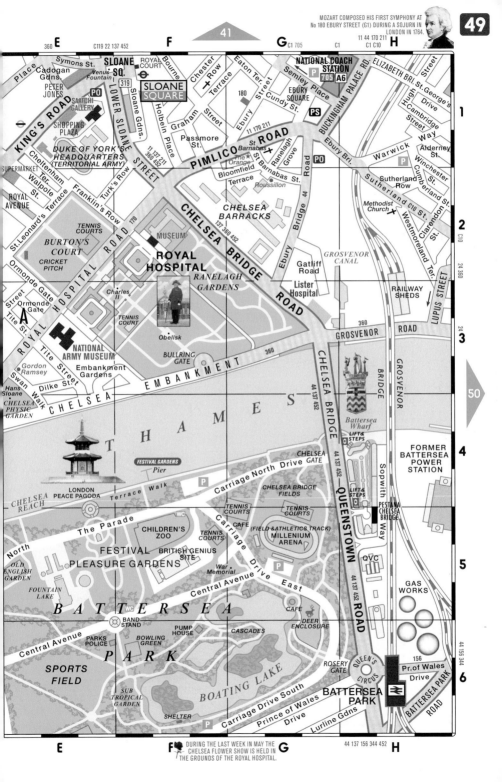

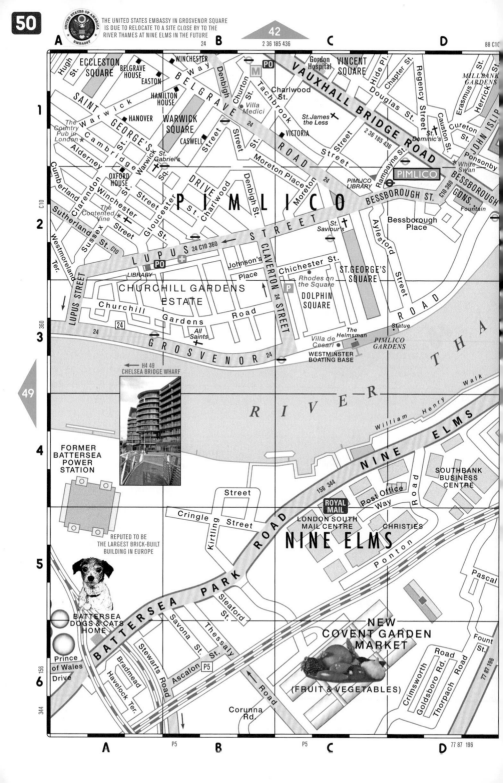

Map labels (Pimlico / Nine Elms area):

Hugh St. · ECCLESTON SQUARE · BELGRAVE HOUSE · EASTON · WINCHESTER Way · CHURTON · TACHBROOK · CHARLWOOD St. · GORDON HOSPITAL · VINCENT SQUARE · Hide Pl. · Chapter St. · Regency St. · MILLBANK GARDENS · Erasmus St. · Herrick St.

SAINT GEORGE'S · Warwick · HAMILTON HOUSE · HANOVER · WARWICK SQUARE · CASWELL · Villa Medici · St.James the Less · VICTORIA · VAUXHALL BRIDGE ROAD · Douglas St. · Causton St. · Cureton St. · Ponsonby · JOHN ISLIP

The Country Pub in London · Cambridge St. · Alderney · St. Gabriel's Sq. · DRIVE · Moreton Place · 2 36 185 436 · St. Dominic's · White Swan · BESSBOROUGH

Cumberland St. · OXFORD HOUSE · Winchester St. · Gloucester St. · Charlwood St. · Denbigh St. · PIMLICO · Moreton · PIMLICO LIBRARY · BESSBOROUGH ST. · GDNS · Fountain

Sutherland St. · Clarendon St. · Sussex St. · The Contented Vine · PIMLICO · St. Saviour's · Bessborough Place

Lupus Street · PO · LIBRARY · LUPUS STREET · Johnson's Place · CLAVERTON STREET · Chichester St. · Rhodes on the Square · ST. GEORGE'S SQUARE · Aylesford St.

CHURCHILL GARDENS ESTATE · Churchill Gardens Road · P · DOLPHIN SQUARE · Statue

GROSVENOR · All Saints · Villa de Cesari · The Helmsman · PIMLICO GARDENS · WESTMINSTER BOATING BASE · ROAD

← H4 49 · CHELSEA BRIDGE WHARF · RIVER THA

49

RIVER · William Henry · Walk · NINE ELMS

FORMER BATTERSEA POWER STATION · Street · 156 344 · Post Office · Road · SOUTHBANK BUSINESS CENTRE

Cringle Street · Kirtling Street · ROYAL MAIL · LONDON SOUTH MAIL CENTRE · Way · CHRISTIES · Ponton

REPUTED TO BE THE LARGEST BRICK-BUILT BUILDING IN EUROPE · NINE ELMS

BATTERSEA DOGS & CATS HOME · Sleaford St. · Savona St. · Thessaly St. · NEW COVENT GARDEN MARKET · Pascal

Prince of Wales Drive · BATTERSEA PARK ROAD · Stewarts Road · Bradmead · Havelock Ter. · Ascalon St. · P5 · Road · (FRUIT & VEGETABLES) · Crimsworth Road · Goldsboro Rd. · Thorpach Road · Fount St. · 77 87 196

Corunna Rd.

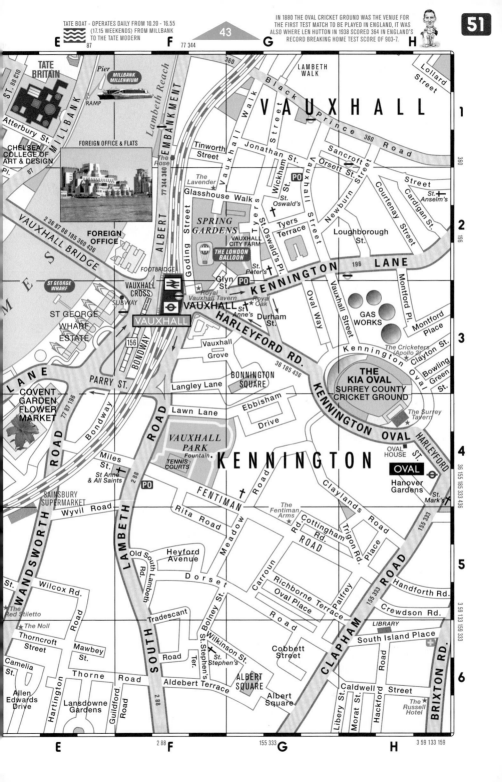

E   F   43   G   H   51

TATE BOAT - OPERATES DAILY FROM 10.20 - 16.55 (17.15 WEEKENDS) FROM MILLBANK TO THE TATE MODERN

87   77 344

IN 1880 THE OVAL CRICKET GROUND WAS THE VENUE FOR THE FIRST TEST MATCH TO BE PLAYED IN ENGLAND, IT WAS ALSO WHERE LEN HUTTON IN 1938 SCORED 364 IN ENGLAND'S RECORD BREAKING HOME TEST SCORE OF 903-7.

VAUXHALL

TATE BRITAIN
Pier
MILLBANK MILLENNIUM
RAMP

LAMBETH WALK

ST. BB C10
Atterbury St.
MILLBANK

CHELSEA COLLEGE OF ART & DESIGN Pl.

FOREIGN OFFICE & FLATS

The Rose

Tinworth Street

Glasshouse Walk

The Lavender

Lambeth Reach

EMBANKMENT

ALBERT

Goding Street

SPRING GARDENS

VAUXHALL CITY FARM
THE LONDON BALLOON

FOOTBRIDGE

Vauxhall Walk

Jonathan St.

Wickham St.

St. Oswald's

St. Oswald's Pl.

Tyers St.

Black Prince Road

360

LAMBETH WALK

Sancroft St.

Orsett St.

Newburn St.

Vauxhall Street

Courtenay Street

Lollard Street

St. Anselm's

Cardigan St.

Street

Loughborough St.

VAUXHALL BRIDGE

2 36 87 88 185 360 436

FOREIGN OFFICE

ST GEORGE WHARF

VAUXHALL CROSS
SUBWAY

VAUXHALL

ST GEORGE WHARF ESTATE

BONDWAY

156

PARRY ST.

Tyers Terrace

St. Peter's

Glyn St.

PO

Royal Vauxhall Tavern

Royal Oak

St Anne's

Durham St.

KENNINGTON

Oval Way

196

LANE

Vauxhall Street

Montford Pl.

GAS WORKS

Montford Place

The Cricketers (Apollo 2)

Clayton St.

Bowling Green St.

HARLEYFORD RD.

Vauxhall Grove

Langley Lane

BONNINGTON SQUARE

36 185 436

Kennington

KENNINGTON OVAL

THE KIA OVAL
SURREY COUNTY CRICKET GROUND

The Surrey Tavern

LANE

COVENT GARDEN FLOWER MARKET

77 87 196

Bondway

Lawn Lane

Ebbisham Drive

VAUXHALL PARK
Fountain.

TENNIS COURTS

KENNINGTON

OVAL HOUSE

OVAL

Hanover Gardens

St. Mark's

HARLEYFORD St.

36 155 185 333 436

WANDSWORTH ROAD

ROAD

Miles

St Anne & All Saints

2 88

PO

SAINSBURY SUPERMARKET

Wyvil Road

FENTIMAN

Rita Road

Meadow Road

The Fentiman Arms

Cottingham Rd.

Claylands Road

Trigon Rd.

Trigon Place

ROAD

155 333

CLAPHAM

Handforth Rd.

Crewdson Rd.

3 59 133 159 333

The Red Stiletto

The Noll

Wilcox Rd.

Road

Old South Lambeth Rd.

Heyford Avenue

D o r s e t

Carroun Road

Richborne Terrace

Oval Place

Palfrey Place

LIBRARY

South Island Place

155 333

Thorncroft Street

Mawbey St.

Thorne Road

ROAD

Binfield St. Stephen's Ter.

Wilkinson St.

St. Stephen's

Cobbett Street

ROAD

Caldwell Street

BRIXTON RD.

Camelia St.

Allen Edwards Drive

Lansdowne Gardens

Hartington Road

Guildford Road

Aldebert Terrace

ALBERT SQUARE

Albert Square

Libery St.

Morat St.

Hackford Road

The Russell Hotel

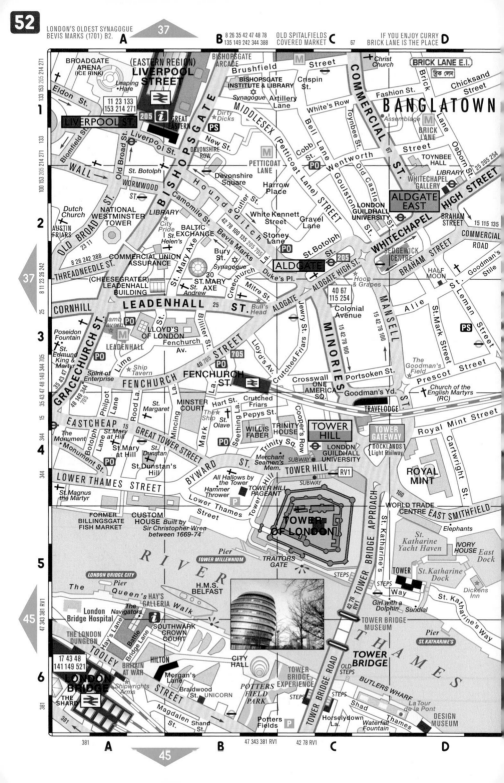

LONDON'S OLDEST SYNAGOGUE
BEVIS MARKS (1701) B2.

A ◄ 37 ►

B 8 26 35 42 47 48 78
135 149 242 344 388

OLD SPITALFIELDS **C**
COVERED MARKET

67

IF YOU ENJOY CURRY **D**
BRICK LANE IS THE PLACE

BROADGATE ARENA (ICE RINK)
Leaping Hare
Eldon St.
133 155 205 214 271
11 23 133
153 214 271
Blomfield St.
Liverpool St.
St. Botolph
Old Broad St.
WALL
100 153 205 214 271
133
WORMWOOD ST.
Dutch Church
AUSTIN FRIARS
NATIONAL WESTMINSTER TOWER
OLD BROAD ST.
23 11
8 26 242 388
THREADNEEDLE ST.
COMMERCIAL UNION ASSURANCE
35 43 47 149 344 705
8 11 23 26 242
CORNHILL
25
POSEIDON FOUNTAIN
St. Edmund King & Martyr
GRACECHURCH ST.
Lamb Tavern
PO
M
LEADENHALL
Spirit of Enterprise
48 344 705
705
EASTCHEAP
15
The Monument
344
Monument St.
Botolph Lane
Philpot Lane
Rood La.
St. Margaret
ST. MARY AT HILL
Lime St.
St. Mary at Hill
St. Dunstan Hill
St. Dunstan's Hill
LOWER THAMES STREET
St. Magnus the Martyr
FORMER BILLINGSGATE FISH MARKET
CUSTOM HOUSE Built by Sir Christopher Wren between 1669-74

(EASTERN REGION)
LIVERPOOL STREET
LIVERPOOL ST.
205
i GREAT EASTERN
PS
Liverpool St.
DEVONSHIRE ROW
New St.
Devonshire Square
LIBRARY
City Pride
St. Helen's
BALTIC EXCHANGE
Bury St.
30 ST. MARY AXE
St. Andrew
COMMERCIAL UNION ASSURANCE
(CHEESEGRATER) LEADENHALL BUILDING
25
LEADENHALL ST.
Bull's Head
Billiter St.
LLOYD'S OF LONDON
Fenchurch Av.
40 705
705
FENCHURCH STREET
Lloyd's Av.
Crutched Friars
Crosswall
ONE AMERICA SQ.
FENCHURCH ST.
MINSTER COURT
The Ship
St. Olave
Pepys St.
Crutched Friars
Mincing La.
Mark La.
Hart St.
GREAT TOWER STREET
Seething La.
WILLIS FABER
TRINITY HOUSE
Trinity Sq.
BYWARD ST.
All Hallows by the Tower
Hammer Thrower
P
TOWER HILL PAGEANT
Lower Thames Street
Tower Bridge Approach

BISHOPSGATE ARCADE
BISHOPSGATE
Brushfield St.
BISHOPSGATE INSTITUTE & LIBRARY
Synagogue
Crispin St.
Artillery Lane
MIDDLESEX (Petticoat Lane) STREET
Dirty Dicks
White's Row
Bell Lane
Cobb La.
PETTICOAT LANE
Harrow Place
Cutler St.
White Kennett Street
Gravel Lane
Stoney Lane
Bevis Marks
St. Mary Axe
Houndsditch
Camomile St.
Duke's Pl.
St. Botolph St.
ALDGATE
Creechurch La.
Mitre St.
Jewry St.
ALDGATE HIGH ST.
205
Aldgate
40 67 115 254
Cooper's Row
Portsoken St.
Goodman's Yd.
Goodman's Stile
TRAVELODGE
Church of the English Martyrs (RC)
Prescot Street
15 42 78 100
MINORIES
MANSELL STREET
TOWER HILL
LONDON GUILDHALL UNIVERSITY
Merchant Seamen's Mem.
RV1
SUBWAY
TOWER HILL
SUBWAY
TOWER OF LONDON
TOWER GATEWAY
DOCKLANDS (Light Railway)
ROYAL MINT
Royal Mint Street
Cartwright St.
WORLD TRADE CENTRE
EAST SMITHFIELD
Elephants

M
Christ Church
BRICK LANE E.I.
ব্রিক লেন
COMMERCIAL ST.
Fashion St.
Brick La.
Chicksand Street
BANGLATOWN
Assemblage
Toynbee St.
Wentworth Street
Old Castle St.
WHITECHAPEL
Goulston St.
ALDGATE EAST
M
BRICK LANE
Osborn St.
TOYNBEE HALL
WHITECHAPEL GALLERY
LIBRARY
HIGH STREET
BRAHAM STREET
15 115 135
COMMERCIAL ROAD
SEDGEWICK CENTRE
HALF MOON
Alie St.
Leman Street
St. Mark Street
Goodman's Field
PS
225 205 254
15 42 78 100

Colonial Avenue
Hoop & Grapes

RIVER THAMES
Pier
TOWER MILLENNIUM
TRAITORS GATE
STEPS
St. Katharine's Way
ST. KATHARINE'S
Pier
St. Katharine Yacht Haven
IVORY HOUSE East Dock
St. Katharine Dock
Dickens Inn
Girl with a Dolphin
Sundial
TOWER
STEPS
TOWER BRIDGE MUSEUM
100
TOWER BRIDGE ROAD
TOWER BRIDGE
BUTLERS WHARF
Shad Thames
La Tour de la Pont
DESIGN MUSEUM
Waterfall Fountain

LONDON BRIDGE CITY
The Queen's Walk
Pier
HAY'S GALLERIA
H.M.S. BELFAST
The Navigators
London Bridge Hospital
i
THE LONDON DUNGEON
TOOLEY
17 43 48
141 149 521
LONDON BRIDGE
THE SHARD
381
Hay's Lane
Battle Bridge Lane
BRITAIN AT WAR
Shipwrights Arms
Morgan's Lane
Braidwood St.
UNICORN
Magdalen St.
Shand St.
SOUTHWARK CROWN COURT
HILTON
CITY HALL
POTTERS FIELDS PARK
TOWER BRIDGE EXPERIENCE
OLD STEPS
Horselydown La.
STEPS
Potters Fields
P

A ◄ 45 ►
381

B
47 343 381 RV1

C
42 78 RV1

D

37 (left margin)
45 (left margin)

THE TOWER OF LONDON

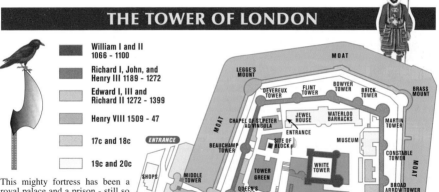

William I and II
1066 - 1100

Richard I, John, and
Henry III 1189 - 1272

Edward I, III and
Richard II 1272 - 1399

Henry VIII 1509 - 47

17c and 18c

19c and 20c

(Map labels: MOAT, LEGGE'S MOUNT, DEVEREUX TOWER, FLINT TOWER, BOWYER TOWER, BRICK TOWER, BRASS MOUNT, CHAPEL OF ST.PETER AD VINCULA, JEWEL HOUSE, WATERLOO BARRACKS, MARTIN TOWER, MOAT, ENTRANCE, BEAUCHAMP TOWER, SITE OF BLOCK, MUSEUM, CONSTABLE TOWER, MOAT, SHOPS, MIDDLE TOWER, TOWER GREEN, WHITE TOWER, BROAD ARROW TOWER, QUEEN'S HOUSE, BYWARD TOWER, BELL TOWER, BLOODY TOWER, WAKEFIELD TOWER, ARMOURIES, LANTHORN TOWER, SALT TOWER, TOWER PIER, QUEEN'S STEPS, TRAITOR'S GATE, ST.THOMAS'S TOWER, MOAT, WELL TOWER, RIVER THAMES, CRADLE TOWER, DEVELIN TOWER, ENTRANCE)

This mighty fortress has been a royal palace and a prison - still so used if necessary - a place of execution, a garrison and armoury, and a stronghold that contains the fabulous Crown Jewels. The great central keep, or White Tower is the oldest building. It was erected by the monk Gundulph, Bishop of Rochester, in 1078 for William the Conqueror in order to protect and overawe the city. The first floor contains the Chapel of St. John, Londons' oldest church. The inner wall, with its 13 towers was added in the 13th century and further additions and alterations were made by successive monarchs.The Queen's House has had amongst its inmates several of Henry VIII's wives, Roger Casement, the Irish revolutionary

and Rudolf Hess, Hitler's deputy. Other notable features to interest the visitor include the Bloody Tower, with its portcullis, where Sir Walter Raleigh began to write his unfinished "History of the World", Traitors' Gate through which state prisoners passed, the Jewel House with the Crown Jewels and the White Tower which contains a wonderful collection of arms and armour - look for HenryVIII's armour for an idea of his real size. On Tower Green is the site of the execution block and the tower ravens. Always here are the Yeoman Warders - Beefeaters - in their traditional uniform.

THE NORMAN
WHITE TOWER
Daily March - Oct 9.00 - 17.00, Suns 10.00 - 17.00.
Nov - Feb 9.00 - 16.00, Suns & Mons 10.00. Charge

RIVER AND CANAL TRIPS

RIVER TRIPS Splendid trips are available on the River Thames during the summer months. In the evenings there are also supper trips for that special family or romantic occasion. These regular boat services run the whole length of the river, from April to October, when they revert to winter schedules. Within the London area there are daily services from Westminster Bridge, upriver to Kew Gardens, Hampton Court, and the riverside at Richmond, and downriver to the Tower of London, Greenwich and the Thames Barrier. Supper cruises also embark from Westminster Pier.

From Charing Cross Pier there are services to and from Tower Bridge and Greenwich.

From the rail terminals at Waterloo and Paddington there are combined Rail-River trips going to and from Windsor, Staines, Maidenhead, Marlow, Oxford and other attractive places along the river.

Full information on these trips is available from
Charing Cross Pier (map ref. F6 35) ☎ 7987 1185
Westminster Pier (F3 43) ☎ 7930 9033
London Tourist Board ☎ 0839 123432

THE THAMES BARRIER This remarkable piece of engineering is the world's largest moveable defense against flooding. Cruises to the flood barrier embark from Westminster Pier and Lambeth Pier stopping at Canary Wharf and Greenwich. ☎ 7930 3373

CANAL TRIPS Frequent waterbus services run on the Regent's Canal by the London Waterbus Company starting from Little Venice, Paddington (G1 31), passing through Regent's Park to the London Zoo.
Inclusive Waterbus and Zoo tickets can be bought.

There are also narrow boat cruises from Blomfield Road (Little Venice) to Camden Lock and from Camden Lock to the Zoo and Little Venice.
London Waterbus Company
Camden Lock, NW1 ☎ 7482 2550
Jason's Trip runs from Little Venice to Camden Lock in an original painted narrow boat along the Grand Union Canal and the Regent's Canal.
Restaurant. Snacks, beer, wine, soft drinks on sale.
Booking Office ☎ 7286 3428
There are "Jenny Wren" cruises on the Regent's Canal in traditionally decorated narrow boats through the Zoo, Regent's Park and Maida Hill tunnel.
250 Camden High Street,NW1 ☎ 7485 4433
The "Fair Lady" narrow boat has a restaurant and runs dinner cruises from Tuesday to Saturday 19.30 or 20.00 hours, and lunch cruises on Sundays 12.30 or 13.00 hours but booking in advance for these is essential at Camden Lock Office.
277 Camden High Street, NW1 ☎ 7485 6210

PLACES OF INTEREST AROUND LONDON

HAMPTON COURT PALACE   Until 1514 a fine country mansion stood on this site in its lovely situation twelve miles down river from Westminster. Then the ascending (at that time) Cardinal Thomas Wolsey acquired the land and the house and began building this elegant and stately palace. When he fell from favour with his royal master Henry VIII he tried to stave off his inevitable downfall by presenting the palace in 1528 to the King - all to no avail, Wolsey died the next year. Henry really enjoyed the palace and moved in with his mistress and "owne darling", Anne Boleyn. He continued sumptuously enlarging the palace: the grounds, the vast kitchens with their huge fireplaces, and he also added tennis courts. Possibly two of the best parts of the original Tudor building commissioned by Henry are the beamed *Great Hall* with its magnificent tapestries and stained-glass windows, and the *Clock Court* which contains the famous *Astronomical Clock* (1540)which was originally in Henry's other palace in St James.

When William and Mary jointly came to the throne in 1689 there were plans afoot to demolish the palace, but fortunately they employed Sir Christopher Wren to enclose the south front and entirely rebuild the east side; within which he created the beautiful cloistered *Fountain Court*. During William's reign *The Maze*, a circular version, was created, later it was replaced by the triangular maze in 1715.

The house has many great paintings and however time-limited you are it is well worth a visit. A noble feature of the gardens is the most famous vine in the world, the vigorous black hamburg grapevine *The Great Vine* planted in 1768 by Capability Brown.

Approached by rail (within Zone 6 if you have a travel card) from Waterloo Station to Hampton Court then a 200 metre walk over the bridge. Perhaps the most interesting approach is by riverboat from Westminster - it can take about 4 hours.

The Gardens are open to the public daily until dusk except Christmas Day.

Palace and Maze Winter November - March Monday to Sunday 10.00 - 16.30.

Summer April - October 10.00 - 18.00 Closed 24th to the 26th December

BUSHY PARK   Across Hampton Court Road lies this 1100-acre former hunting park still containing over 300 deer. Near the Hampton Court gate you will see the *Diana Fountain* (1713) and beyond for one mile *Chestnut Avenue*, a vista to behold in spring. During WW2 Bushy was the US 8th Army headquarters for Operation Overlord in 1944, with General Eisenhower, supreme commander.

HENRY VIII BY HANS HOLBEIN

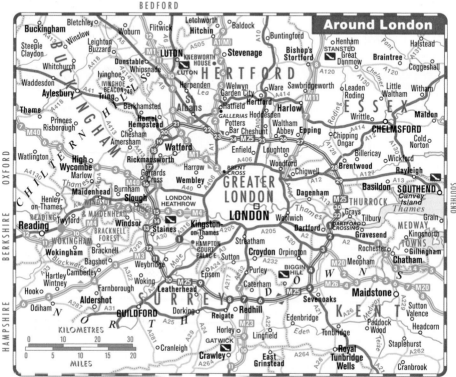

HATFIELD HOUSE and BISHOP'S PALACE

Main Gate situated opposite Hatfield Station.   Acquired by Henry VIII after the Dissolution, the old Palace built in 1485 became a home for his children. Later Elizabeth I was confined to the palace by her sister Mary Tudor who was at that time Queen. The splendid Jacobean house was built by Robert Cecil, the first Earl of Salisbury, between 1607-12, he had exchanged with James I, Theobalds Park for the Palace. All that remains of the Palace is one wing, which was made into stables, and is now used as a restaurant with occasional Elizabethan banquets. The house has many fine paintings, furniture, armour, tapestries and relics dating back to the 15th century. The Marble Hall which takes up the width of the Jacobean house contains two paintings of Elizabeth I, both are exquisite. On the Grand Staircase there is a painting of a horse which is reputed to have been ridden by Elizabeth to review her troops before the Spanish Armada. Elizabeth's gardening hat, gloves and silk stockings will no doubt interest followers of fashion. The gardens are worth a visit in their own right to see the work of the famous 17th century gardening botanists - father and son, both named John Tradescant. A Festival of Gardening is held on the third weekend in June.
Easter Saturday - 30th September 12.00 - 17.00,
Wednesday to Sunday and Bank Holidays.   *Charge*

KEW GARDENS A lovely 300-acre park and arboretum adjacent to the River Thames, ten miles from Central London with stately tree-lined avenues and sequestered walks. The many features to peruse include: a *Chinese Pagoda* (164 foot high), a *Japanese Gateway (*a smaller version of a Buddhist Temple gate in Kyoto), Conservatories, a *Palm House,* an *Orangery,* and the latest addition a *Woodland Walk* 18 metres high, 200 metres long opened in 2008 - it safely moves and sways in the wind! Whether you go when the bluebells are out or the daffodils are blooming, any season holds unknown surprises - for me the glorious rhododenderon trees in bloom is always a good time to visit.

THE PALM HOUSE

Take the District Line tube to Kew Gardens Station then walk down Lichfield Road to the Victoria Gate entrance.
Open *Winter 9.30-16.15, except 24th-25th December, Summer 9.30-18.30, weekends 19.30. Children go free / Charge*

CLOCK TOWER
ST ALBANS

ST. ALBANS Steeped in history: a Celtic settlement *Verlamion* long before the Romans arrived and built their town and a theatre by the River Ver. In AD 61 it was set on fire by the warrior Queen Boudiccca. On the hill where the Abbey stands today, a Roman called Alban became the first Christian martyr to die in Britain.
It is difficult to believe, but underneath the rolling hills of *Verulamium Park* is another Pompeii. In the park there are several outcrops of the *Roman Wall* and a *Hypocaust* which shows you the underfloor heating system the Romans used. Across the way from the superb unmissable *Verulamium Museum* are the remains of the Roman theatre on the Gorhambury estate: a lovely walk takes you to the original ruined *Gorhambury House* where Sir Francis Bacon and his father before him lived. After the martyrdom of Alban, a Saxon church stood on the hill: parts of this church were incorporated into the transept of the Norman abbey which became the focal point of a large monastery. There is so much to relate concerning *St Albans Abbey:* the first draft of Magna Carta was read here, the ceiling of the central tower with red and white roses depicts the Church's ambiguous approach to the Wars of the Roses - the opening battle was fought in St. Albans.
At the bottom of the hill at the side of the River Ver is the *Fighting Cocks,* a 'Medieval Dovecote' built over a former monastery building in 1600 and recognised as the oldest inhabited public house in the country officially accepted and entered in the Guinness Book of Records. The name reflects one of its previous attractions. *St. Albans is 35 minutes from St Pancras on a fast train or try the*
uno *bus 712 or 714 from Victoria Coach Station or Marble Arch which takes approximately 75 minutes.*   *Do check the Official Bus Time Tables*

ABBEY AND FIGHTING COCKS BY RONALD MADDOX

KNEBWORTH HOUSE

Accessed from the A1(M) Externally the palatial building is Victorian Gothic, the figment of author Edward Bulwer-Lytton's imagination. It is though much more than that. The magnificent Banqueting Hall partly dates from the Jacobean period and contains a 1930s painting by Winston Churchill of the hall; private theatricals were performed here by a group led by Charles Dickens. The Library contains many Lytton family treasures including a unique Dutch musical clock. The Lytton family had connections with India, and the British Raj exhibition, housed in a former squash court, contains many mementoes.
The features of the original gardens are gradually being restored and include a rose garden, sunken lawn and a maze. For the family there is a narrow gauge railway, adventure playground and picnic areas.
Knebworth is renowned for its medieval jousting tournaments, and concerts of great jazz, rock and pop artists during the summer months.   *Guided Tours of the House only.*
Open Daily from early April - end of September.   *Charge*
Park, Gardens,Playground and Railway 11.00 -17.30 House & Indian Raj Display 12.00-17.00

56

A H3 B C H3 D

CYCLE TRACKS

1

RAILWAY WORKS

TENNIS COURTS

Chandos Way

WC PAVILION

HAMPSTEAD HEATH

(PRIVATE) TURNER'S WOOD

Ingram Avenue K3

Wildwood Road

THE BISHOP'S AVENUE

LANE

SPORTS GROUND

NORTH WOOD

EAST LODGE

Winnington Road

H3 210 603

QUARRY

WEST LODGE

Ivy Arch

WC

NORTH END ROAD

West Heath Avenue

Wellgarth Rd.

H3 Way

Park Av.

Park Drive

The Park

IVY HOUSE
(Anna Pavlova lived here)

STONE BRIDGE

LILY POND

YHA HOSTEL

KING ALFRED SCHOOL

Manor House Hospital

Hampstead Way

Seven Sisters Ponds

Drinking Fountain

IKINS CORNER

210 268

WC

Golders Hill Girl

CAFETERIA

Olde Bull & Bush

North End

Wildwood Rd.

Spaniards Close

FARM HOUSE

Empyrian
(Barbara Hepworth)

P

LIME WALK

STEPS

THE IVEAGH BEQUEST
(KENWOOD HOUSE)

Two Piece Reclining Figure
(Henry Moore)

KENWOOD

Wood Pond

The Spaniards Inn

OLD TOLL HOUSE

WEST MEADOW

STONE BRIDGE

KEN WOOD ICE HOUSE

DUELLING GROUND

2

TENNIS

GOLDERS HILL PARK

WATER GARDEN

ANIMAL AND BIRD ENCLOSURES

Golders Hill

BANDSTAND

STEPS

DEER

North End Avenue

PITT'S GARDEN

SANDY HEATH

HEATH END

MOUNT TYNDAL

THE ELMS

THE ELMS GARDEN

SPRINGETT'S WOOD

SPHAGNUM BOG

BEECH MOUNT

HAMPSTEAD GATE

WEST FIELD GATE

HAMPST

SOUTH

3

Sandy Road

ADVENTURE PLAYGROUND

THE HILL GARDEN

THE PERGOLA

INVERFORTH HOUSE

THE PADDOCK

BANK HOLIDAY FAIRGROUND

Round Cottage

WC

EAST HEATH

VIADUCT BRIDGE

Viaduct Pond

Shelter

SPORTS GROUND

BRIDGE

HEAT

Leg of Mutton Pond

WEST HEATH

Spring

West Heath Road

HEATH HOUSE

Jack Straw's Castle

P

Flagpole

War Memorial

THE POUND

Vale of Health

Vale of Health Pond

VALE OF HEALTH

PRYORS FIELD

4

APPROX. MAGNETIC NORTH

Platt's Lane

Rosecroft Av.

Hollycroft Av.

Redington Road

Templewood Avenue

VIADUCT BRIDGE (D3)

West Heath Rd.

Whitestone Pond

Branch Hill

ADMIRAL'S HOUSE

Lower Terrace

Upper Terrace

Windmill Hill

FROGNAL RISE

FENTON HOUSE

Holford Road

Squire's Mount

Cannon Pl.

Christ Church

Duke of Hamilton

East Heath Road

Cannon Lane

Christchurch

Well Walk

Wells Tavern

Well Road

LOWER FAIRGROUND

P

5

Ferncroft Avenue

Croft Way

Kidderpore Gardens

Kidderpore Avenue

Heath Drive

Bracknell Gardens

Oakhill Avenue

Greenaway Gdns.

Oak Hill Way

Frognal

Chesterford Gardens

Frognal Gdns.

Church Row

St. John's

Mt. Vernon

Holly Walk

St. Mary's

Holly Hill

Three Horse Shoes

Le Cellier du Midi

John Harrison

New End

Ye Olde White Bear

Flask Walk

STEPS

Streatley Pl.

New End Sq.

NEW HAMPSTEAD

BURGH HO.

Hampstead Museum

HAMPSTEAD

The Flask

Gayton Rd.

Rudall Cres.

Carlingford Rd.

Kemplay Rd.

King of Bohemia

Byrons

Denning Rd.

Willow Rd.

No.2 WILLOW RD.

Freemasons Arms

Pilgrim's Lane

Downshire Hill

St. John's

Keats Grove

KEAT'S HOUSE MUSEUM

PREACHER'S HILL

P

PO

6

St. Andrew's

Langland Gardens

Lindfield Gardens

Finchley Hill

Cannon Hill

PO

Honeybourne Road

Crediton Hill

FINCHLEY ROAD

13 82 113

West End Lane

Alvanley Gdns.

Lymington Rd.

HAMPSTEAD CRICKET CLUB

Fawley Rd.

UNIVERSITY COLLEGE SCHOOL

CAMDEN ARTS CENTRE

Arkwright Road

THEATRE

Frognal Lane

Frognal

King William IV

EVERYMAN

Mt. Vernon

Church Row

JOHN CONSTABLE Tomb

Ellerdale Rd.

Prince Arthur Rd.

FITZJOHN'S AVENUE

HAMPSTEAD

HIGH ST.

46 268

Gayton

PO

PRIMARY SCHOOL

Netherhall Gardens

SCHOOL

Lyndhurst Terrace

Thurlow Road

Maresfield Gardens

SIGMUND FREUD
1856–1939
founder of Psychoanalysis
Lived here in 1938–39

Netherhall Way

Netherhall Gardens

Belsize Crescent

Daleham Gdns.

Belsize Avenue

Lyndhurst Gardens

Akenside Road

Wedderburn Lane

Lyndhurst Gardens

Eldon Grove

FORMER CHURCH

Perceval Av.

Belsize Lane

Ornan Rd.

ROSSLYN HILL

Hampstead Hill Gdns.

THE HOUSE HOTEL

The Roebuck

PS

Keats Hurst

Pond St.

PO

PREMIER TRAVEL INN

268

FINCHLEY RD. & FROGNAL

A B 13 82 113 C D 268

TO FREUD MUSEUM
20 MARESFIELD GARDENS
WEDNESDAY - SUNDAY 12.00 17.00 CHARGE

46 603 HAMPSTEAD STATION HAS THE DEEPEST
LIFT SHAFT (55.2 METRES) ON
THE UNDERGROUND SYSTEM.

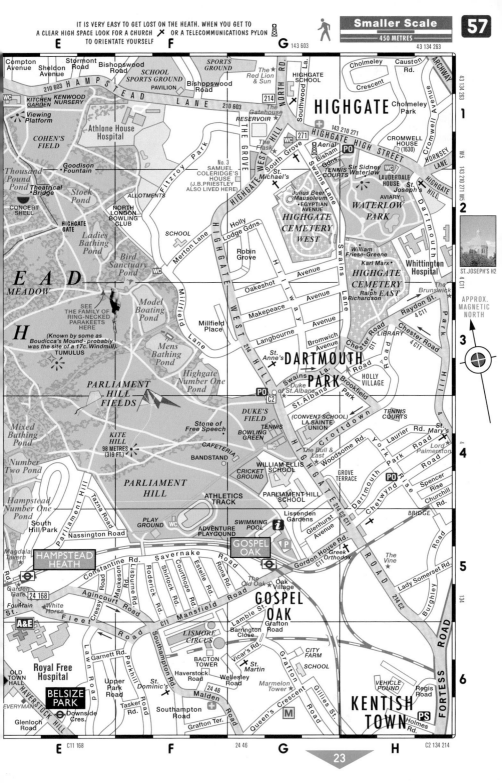

THE LONDON ZOO

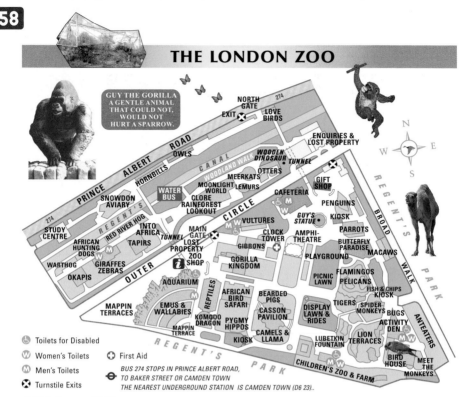

GUY THE GORILLA
A GENTLE ANIMAL
THAT COULD NOT,
WOULD NOT
HURT A SPARROW.

NORTH GATE
EXIT
LOVE BIRDS
ENQUIRIES & LOST PROPERTY
OWLS
ROAD
ALBERT
CANAL
WOODLAND WALK
WOODEN DINOSAUR
TUNNEL
HORNBILLS
PRINCE
MEERKATS
OTTERS
MOONLIGHT WORLD
LEMURS
GIFT SHOP
WATER BUS
CLORE RAINFOREST LOOKOUT
CAFETERIA
SNOWDON AVIARY
PENGUINS
REGENT'S
CIRCLE
GUY'S STATUE
KIOSK
REGENT'S
BROAD
WALK
PARK
STUDY CENTRE
INTO AFRICA
RED RIVER HOG
TUNNEL
MAIN GATE
VULTURES
CLOCK TOWER
AMPHI-THEATRE
PARROTS
AFRICAN HUNTING DOGS
TAPIRS
LOST PROPERTY
GIBBONS
BUTTERFLY PARADISE
MACAWS
WARTHOG
GIRAFFES ZEBRAS
ZOO SHOP
GORILLA KINGDOM
PLAYGROUND
FLAMINGOS
OKAPIS
OUTER
AQUARIUM
PICNIC LAWN
PELICANS
REPTILES
AFRICAN BIRD SAFARI
BEARDED PIGS
DISPLAY LAWN & RIDES
FISH & CHIPS KIOSK
MAPPIN TERRACES
EMUS & WALLABIES
CASSON PAVILION
TIGERS
SPIDER MONKEYS
BUGS
KOMODO DRAGON
PYGMY HIPPOS
ACTIVITY DEN
ANTEATERS
MAPPIN TERRACE
CAMELS & LLAMA
LION TERRACES
REGENT'S
KIOSK
LUBETKIN FOUNTAIN
BIRD HOUSE
MEET THE MONKEYS
PARK
CHILDREN'S ZOO & FARM

Toilets for Disabled

Women's Toilets   First Aid

Men's Toilets

Turnstile Exits

BUS 274 STOPS IN PRINCE ALBERT ROAD,
TO BAKER STREET OR CAMDEN TOWN
THE NEAREST UNDERGROUND STATION IS CAMDEN TOWN (D6 23)..

Grid Reference F2 25

The London Zoo is one of the oldest and most famous animal collections in the world, and, together with Whipsnade Park in Bedfordshire, forms part of the Zoological Society of London, a scientific society founded by Sir Stamford Raffles and others in 1826. The zoo extends over an area of 36 acres in Regent's Park. More than 12,000 animals live here, including lions, giraffes, gorillas, and many other species of mammals together with birds, reptiles, amphibians, fishes and insects. A high proportion of the animals were born here but many others come from other zoos throughout the world.

I loved this zoo as a child and still do try to visit London and Whipsnade twice a year. My father always had a particular fascination for the gentle gorillas and *Guy* in particular, who always gave you that quizzical look, weighing you up as much as you were him. Alas he is long gone, as is my father, but *Guy's* statue stands in the zoo and always jogs my memory of happy bygone days.

The Gorilla Kingdom is the lushly vegetated habitat for the west lowland gorillas, colobus monkeys, rainforest birds, and lizards; while the new Clore Rainforest Lookout has tropical trees, monkeys, birds, tiny tamarins, marmosets, and iguanas etc.

The hot-pool in the Casson Pavilion is where the pygmy hippos reside in winter: the building also houses camels and llamas. On the Mappin Terraces are emus and wallabies; underneath these terraces is the Aquarium which stretches for 150 yards, (Britains largest), with fishes from fresh, sea, and tropical waters all over the world. Seawater in the circulation system is topped up annually when it is brought in by road-tanker from the North Sea. Here you find deadly piranha fish with razor-sharp teeth, gently drifting seahorses, poisonous dragon fish, eels; all major groups of reptiles are represented - turtles

and terrapins, tortoises, crocodiles and alligators, brilliant coloured and camouflaged lizards, and snakes from the venomous to the benign, with vipers, pythons and boa constrictors.

Animal feeding times are staggered throughout the day and many visitors like to plan their passage through the zoo taking account of these times. Check the timetable when you enter the zoo.

The penguins always look important and are a favourite to watch. I like the way they move along in a queue-like procession, as though waiting for the bus back to Antarctica. They no longer inhabit the Lubetkin pool; this listed architectural delight, with spiral interlocking ramps was designed back in the 1930's by Berthold Lubetkin, today it has a featured fountain. The present penguin habitat is without a concrete base, so it is less toil on their feet!

A marvellous improvement are the Lion Terraces, the cats now live in open areas, rich with plants and grasses that reflect their natural habitat. Inside the Bird House are many beautiful species, including brilliant coloured parakeets, big beaked toucans and hornbills. The largest birds in the world (ostriches and storks) are found in the African Bird Safari enclosure. Guaranteed to make you shudder, the BUGS House contains great colonies of ants, praying mantises, stick insects, spiders and scorpions.

A particularly fascinating collection of creatures is assembled in the Moonlight World where assimilated 'night' is created to encourage nocturnal animals to become active in normal daytime. There are badgers, bush babies, flying foxes, lorises and douroucouli, the only nocturnal monkey in the world.

Open daily except Christmas Day.
Summer 10.00 - 17.30 April - September.
Winter 10.00 - 16.00.   *Charge*

LONDON'S PARKS AND VILLAGES

London is made especially beautiful by the wealth of its green open spaces, and its majestic squares that break the monotony of the grey buildings with their lovely flower-filled gardens. The largest and principal London parks are the Royal Parks, which are Crown property and are open to the public free.

The Royal Parks

THE GREEN PARK Located between Piccadilly and Constitution Hill, this is a relaxing park that is full of mature trees and grassland.

HYDE PARK With the adjoining Kensington Gardens, the park extends to 600 acres of grassland, trees and flower beds, with the Serpentine Lake for boating and fishing (only with a permit), and at the Lido, bathing. restaurants, band concerts, horse riding in Rotten Row, football, bowling and putting.

KENSINGTON GARDENS A former hunting ground laid out by William III, adjoining the west side of Hyde Park and creating a complete contrast - it is a more pleasant and peaceful place. There are Italian Gardens, the Round Pond for model boating, Long Water, the Peter Pan statue and the Albert Memorial.

PRIMROSE HILL From the summit of this grassy hill which is 68 metres (206ft) above sea level, there is a superb panorama of London. An engraved plaque identifies the buildings for you.

REGENT'S PARK A truly lovely park, framed by the beautiful terraced architecture of John Nash who designed this park at the request of the Prince Regent (later George IV). A rose garden, magnificent shrubs and trees, lawns, fountains, rowing on the lake, band concerts, the magical Open-Air Theatre and the Zoo are all part of this great park.

ST. JAMES'S PARK A one time deer park and now very beautiful with a picturesque bridge over an ornamental lake. Many wildfowl, pelicans and geese, fine views and band concerts.

Public Parks and Spaces

BATTERSEA PARK On the southside of the Thames, and the scene of the annual Easter parade. The Peace Pagoda (E5 49) was built in 1985 by Japanese monks to commemorate the tragic bombing of Hiroshima.

HAMPSTEAD HEATH They call the heath 'the lungs of London' and so it is. The heath is 792 acres of pure joy, great for flying kites, for walks through dells and uplands, for woods and unusual fauna. There are lakes for model boats, and swimming and fishing; animal enclosures and ornamental gardens: the Hill Garden (B3 56) with its pergola is well worth seeking out. On summer evenings Kenwood is a lovely setting for the open air Lakeside concerts from opera companies and symphony orchestras.
I always enjoy a brisk walk over the heath with my wife after the excesses of Christmas.

HOLLAND PARK In the heart of Kensington and for the early part of the 20th century, a private garden. Includes a Japanese garden and an open air theatre.

WATERLOW PARK A favourite park of mine situated on top of Highgate Hill. Undulating, small and interesting at every turn, with recreational features, an aviary and Lauderdale House for musical events - classical and jazz.

THE ROOF GARDENS In Kensington near Derry Street (E3 39) on the very top of a building that used to be occupied by Derry & Toms there is an absolutely magnificent and unique rooftop paradise garden; for two days (Thurs. & Sats.) a club and restaurant. Owned by Richard Branson, you can view this when there are no functions.

London's Villages

Before the 19th century and the expansion of the railways London was contained within the City, Westminster and Southwark. The communities that were outside these areas were villages. As transport extended, the villages became a part of the conurbation. Here are a few of the villages that are still discernible within the great conurbation.

HAMPSTEAD Page 56-57. When you arrive at Hampstead on the underground you are 64 metres below ground level in the deepest station in London, and on reaching the surface you know you are in a different atmosphere. For many years, Hampstead has been a haven for arts of all descriptions. John Constable who did many paintings of the heath is buried in the churchyard of St.John's (B5 56), as is John Harrison, the self-taught clockmaker who is attributed with defining 'Longitude' by means of his chronometer. The flagpole (B3 56) at the top of Heath Street is the highest point in London, although the best view is from the top of Parliament Hill. Legends of the highwayman, Dick Turpin, are rife in old pubs like *The Spaniards*, while many of the little back streets reveal surprising architecture mixed in with the cottages. There are numerous cafes and bistros and the fresh air on the heath is therapeutic.

Kenwood House On the north side of the heath is this 17th century Robert Adam house, which has a fine collection of paintings, a Rembrandt self-portrait and works by Turner, Romney, Vermeer, Hals etc. The superb Adam Library is a feature worth looking out for.   *Daily April - Sept 10.00 - 18.00 October - March 10.00 - 16.00   Free*

HIGHGATE Page 57.   Highgate has even more of a village atmosphere. Perched on the top of a hill, it deceptively seems higher than its near neighbour Hampstead. I have already mentioned Waterlow Park which is extremely pleasant, particularly during the week. The famous pub is *The Flask* (G1 57), which dates back to 1767.

On summer evenings the tables are filled with people enjoying the ale and food. John Betjeman loved the pub and they do say that Major Rogers, the frontiersman of 'Rogers Rangers' fame drank here - do you remember Spencer Tracy in the film *Northwest Passage?* Strangely, the biggest attraction in Highgate is the cemetery, for here Karl Marx was put to rest - his memorial is very striking and strong as though it was made forever. In the village there are many international restaurants.

ISLINGTON Page 28 . Home of many intellectuals and artists, not as ostentatious as Chelsea and always full of life. It has an antique shop mall and an antiques market; some great and famous fringe pub theatres like the *King's Head* (B1 28), where often a future West End or Broadway production can be seen in embryo form; the pub still rings your bar bill up in old shillings and pence! Islington is always enjoyable: there are many cafes and restaurants serving every cuisine imaginable: *Le Mercury*, the atmospheric *Cuba Libre* and Mexican *Desperados* (in its previous guise Tony Blair dined here) are all in Upper Street and serve excellent food that will not break your pocket; for more formal dining, *Frederick's* may suit you more. The Victorian pub, the *Camden Head*, has great atmosphere and good lunches (B1 28), and is also a comedy venue.

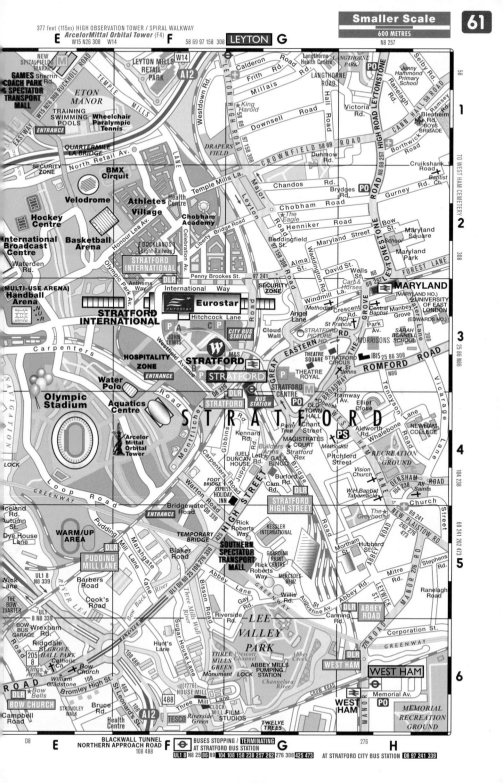

Just like the Lower East Side of New York, the East End of London was always a melting pot of cultures - people came from all over Europe seeking work and to improve their way of life. During the 16th and 17th centuries, Huguenots (Calvinist Protestants) fleeing from religious persecution arrived from France. Later in the 1780s many Chinese sailors working for the East India company docked in the Port of London (once the largest port in the world), they settled in Limehouse and worked in the docks. In the 20th century the area was often featured in films. I remember a musical with the song *'Limehouse Blues'* danced to a backdrop of a foggy mysterious London inhabited by pig-tailed Chinese men and women smoking opium - the film was *Ziegfeld Follies* - in the scene Fred Astaire was a chinaman.

In 1740-41 the aftermath of the first Irish Famine brought large numbers of Irish men to the East End looking for work as labourers or dock-hands; their women went into the sweated labour garment trade or as domestic servants. A hundred years later the failure of the potato crop brought another famine to Ireland forcing more Irish to emmigrate.

The area was always a haven for refugees from oppresion: towards the end of the 19th century an influx of poor Jews from Poland and Russia arrived, some of them used it as a stopover on their way to New York. Today in the East End there are numerous immigrants from Bangladesh and India; if you enjoy curry you can have a feast in Banglatown (D1 52).

With the arrival of the Olympic Games the area has had a huge makeover and is destined for a magnificent party in 2012.

HOUSE MILL / CLOCK MILL   F6 61

Historically known as *Three Mills* and supplying a local Abbey which Henry VIII destroyed, the mills were famous in the 16th century not only for the quality of the flour which was supplied to the City bakers but also for grinding gunpowder. By the 17th century they were producing maize and barley for distillation. Reduced to two mills, the *House Mill* was rebuilt in 1776; the other Mill was rebuilt with a Bell and a Clock in 1817. Through to 1941 they were famous for making an east-end delight or 'mother's ruin'-*Lamplighter Gin*. During WW2 the miller's house was bomb damaged and was rebuilt in 1995 with the original façade and a modern interior. Close by are Three Mills Film Studios making films for TV and cinemas.
House Mill escorted tours Sunday afternoons May to October 13.00-16.00   Charge (children free)
The café opens Mons - Fris 10.00-15.00

THE GEFFRYE MUSEUM   H2 29

Kingsland Road, E2 8EA. An interesting collection of decorative arts and furniture in eleven period settings from 1600 onwards: housed in the original tree-shaded ironmonger's almshouses - fourteen one-storey buildings set around a forecourt, built in 1715 for the old and infirm. It is significant that the museum is situated in an area that at one time was renowned for furniture making.
Tues-Sats 10.00-17.00.   Closed Mondays
Sundays & Bank Holidays 12.00-17.00   Charge

SUTTON HOUSE NATIONAL TRUST   A2 60

2-4 Homerton High Street, Hackney. Unbelievably a Tudor house in the East End that has suvived since 1535. Built by a member of Henry VIII's court, Sir Ralph Sadleir, the atmosphere of past times pervades the oak-panelled rooms in which former occupants, merchants and Huguenot silkweavers, lived at one time.
Open Mons,Tues,Weds 25th July-11th Aug 10.00-16.30
Thurs, Fris 3rd Feb-16th Dec 10.00-16.30
Sats, Suns 5th Feb-18th Dec 12.00-16.30   Charge

THE V&A MUSEUM OF CHILDHOOD   A6 60

Cambridge Heath Road, E2 9PA. Opened in 1872 the Bethnal Green Museum only attained its present purpose in 1973 when the V & A Museum transferred all its child-related exhibits to this subsidiary building. In capacious and light surroundings the permanent exhibits are arranged in three galleries: Moving and Optical toys, Creativity (inspiration - explore - make it happen), Childhood (relating experiences past and present). Distorting mirrors still provide constant amusement for young and old. Adults and children can relate using interactive exhibits.
Five minutes walk from Bethnal Green (Central Line) Tube station. Daily 10.00-17.45. The first Thursday of the month some galleries open until 21.00.   Free

ENTERTAINMENTS

THEATRE ROYAL STRATFORD EAST   **G3 61**
Gerry Raffles Square, E15 1BN   ☎ *020 8985 2424*
Built in 1884, the theatre was extended seven years later
to make it one of the longest of all London stages.
The large stage was used to great advantage when
Joan Littlewood arrived with her Theatre Workshop
Company in 1953. Surviving fires and the bombing
during WW2, the theatre was revitalized on Joan's arrival.

Oh! What a Lovely War was her most famous creation
at the theatre, and was made into a film by Richard
Attenborough. She directed and inspired many other
productions between 1953-79. Art and culture have
flourished since her time with this theatre.

STRATFORD CIRCUS   **G3 61**
Theatre Square, E15 1BX   ☎ *0844 357 2625*
Just a stone-throw from the Olympic Stadium. A
contemporary performing arts venue which features:
music, comedy, dance, jazz, cabaret and children's theatre.
Reached by Central or Jubilee Line tube to Stratford

HACKNEY EMPIRE
291 Mare Street, E8 1EJ   ☎ *020 8534 8381*
This is a beautifully refurbished theatre thanks to the
efforts of Alan Sugar, the billionaire entrepreneur and
star of the TV progamme *The Apprentice*. The listed
building is a former music hall: designed by the
great Frank Matcham, the architect who designed the
London Palladium and the Coliseum. The interior is really
sumptuous; Marie Lloyd, WC Fields, Charlie Chaplin and
Stan Laurel all performed on this stage. Quick rotating
programme changes bring an eclectic mix of comedy,
Shakespeare, jazz, plays, and ballet, and opera from major
touring companies from all over the world to the stage
of this theatre.
*Approached by Central Line tube to Bethnal Green, then
10 minutes by bus 106 or 254.*

VICTORIA PARK

A walk along the streets surrounding
the park proves that this area was
once a very fashionable place to live -
and it still is. Since 1845 it has been
affectionately called the *People's Park,*
and has been the principal open-space
in the East End ever since. Its appeal is
enhanced by being bounded on the west
by the *Regent's Canal* and by the connecting
Hertford Union Canal on the southern edge
where colourful house-boats glide elegantly by.
The central lawn or *Lido Field* was often used

as a place for oratory. Like Speakers Corner in Hyde Park it attracted lively political and religious soap-box speechmakers,
often accompanied by the ever funny hecklers! In more recent years the park has hosted numerous pop-concerts and
has occasionally been the starting point of demonstrations.
Summer or winter the park is a sports place, with large areas for football, rugby, three all-weather cricket pitches, a
three-laned cricket-net where you are free to practise batting strokes and bowling; an athletics track, tennis courts and
a bowling green. The wide pathways are excellent for skating and keep-fit jogging.
Young children also have many delights to enjoy: the pool's playground, a paddling
pool, a deer enclosure, and the model boating lake which hosts an annual regatta
on Easter Sunday. There are several very interesting features to look out for when
you meander through this very underrated - by outsiders - park: the *West Lake*
with its spouting fountain - and - perhaps when you read this you will be able
to see the new lottery funded *Pagoda* in the lake. The *Drinking Fountain* has
a strangely Moorish look, it was donated by Baroness Angela Burdett-Coutts, a
truly amazing woman of the 19th century - a philanthropist, the wealthiest woman
in England, and well ahead of her time. Charles Dickens dedicated *Martin
Chuzzlewit* to her. Burdett-Coutts dispersed her money not only at home but to
charities world-wide.

On the east side of the park are two alcoves which were originally erected on
the old London Bridge and saved after it was demolished in 1831. By the *Crown
Gates* and the *West Lake* is the *Lakeside Pavilion & Cafeteria* which serves organic
food; also there are a number of good pubs encompassing the park.

DOCKLANDS

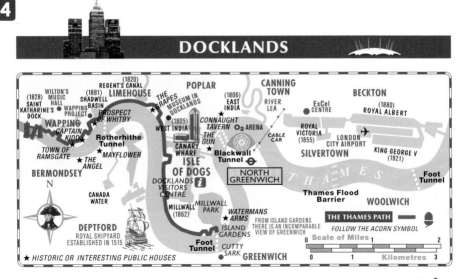

DOCKLANDS

(1820)
REGENT'S CANAL
WILTON'S
(1828) MUSIC (1881) SHADWELL LIMEHOUSE
SAINT HALL BASIN
KATHARINE'S WAPPING THE RAPES
DOCK PROJECT PROSPECT MUSEUM IN
WAPPING OF WHITBY DOCKLANDS
CAPTAIN
KIDD Rotherhithe
TOWN OF Tunnel
RAMSGATE MAYFLOWER
THE
ANGEL
BERMONDSEY
N
CANADA
WATER
DEPTFORD
ROYAL SHIPYARD
ESTABLISHED IN 1515

POPLAR
(1806)
EAST
INDIA
(1805)
WEST INDIA CONNAUGHT
TAVERN O₂ ARENA
THE
GUN
CANARY
WHARF Blackwall
ISLE Tunnel
OF DOGS
DOCKLANDS ℹ
VISITORS
CENTRE NORTH
GREENWICH
MILLWALL
MILLWALL PARK
(1862) WATERMANS
ARMS FROM ISLAND GARDENS
ISLAND THERE IS AN INCOMPARABLE
GARDENS VIEW OF GREENWICH
Foot
Tunnel CUTTY
SARK GREENWICH

CANNING
TOWN
RIVER
LEA ExCel
CENTRE BECKTON
(1880)
ROYAL ALBERT
ROYAL
VICTORIA
CABLE (1855) LONDON
CAR CITY AIRPORT
SILVERTOWN KING GEORGE V
(1921)
Foot
T H A M E S Tunnel
Thames Flood
Barrier WOOLWICH
THE THAMES PATH
FOLLOW THE ACORN SYMBOL
Scale of Miles 1 2
0 1 Kilometres 3

★ HISTORIC OR INTERESTING PUBLIC HOUSES

DOCKLANDS
LIGHT RAILWAY
TOWER
GATEWAY BANK
SHADWELL
LIMEHOUSE
WESTFERRY
WEST INDIA DOCK
CANARY WHARF
HERON QUAYS
SOUTH QUAY
CROSSHARBOUR
MUDCHUTE
ISLAND GARDENS
CUTTY SARK
GREENWICH
DEPTFORD BRIDGE
ELVERSON ROAD
LEWISHAM

The Canary Wharf Tower with its pyramid top, fifty storeys, exterior of stainless steel and height of 800 feet dominates London's skyline: its red flashing light tells you that this is Docklands. The architect is Cesar Pelli, whose other major achievement was the tragic twin towered World Trade Center in New York. The tower is the apex and the centre of the regeneration area on the Isle of Dogs which now harbours some of the finest modern architecture and planning to be seen in London. The best way to reach the area is by the Docklands Light Railway, which takes you directly to Canary Wharf. At this moment in time it is no Manhattan; it is a daytime, working place, where most of the national newspapers have taken roots (in spite of massive opposition from their work forces). For evening pleasures and other activities you have to go up river, but they are working on it.

THE DOCKS The docks, or the old Port of London used to begin to the east of Tower Bridge, and they stretched down river to North Woolwich. Although their history goes back a long time. It was 1515 when an important phase began; Henry VIII established the Royal Shipyards at Deptford and Woolwich. Wide-spread expansion followed during Queen Elizabeth I's reign, which heralded the rise of London as the world's leading financial centre. The growth of empire, steam-engines and industry of the Victorian era created the need for the new deep water docks, and warehouses which were built to accomodate the huge increase of commerce in the area. The construction site at that time was the biggest ever known. In 1940 Hitler tried to annihilate the docklands. He did not succeed, although he caused great damage: some of the old sugar warehouses burned for many days.

BORN AGAIN The end of the docks came in the 1970's with the advent of new technology: containers, mechanical handling, and roll on/off terminals did away with the majority of dockers. Today, the area is more middle class as city workers move into the renovated iron and brick warehouses. They have their own computer controlled driverless overhead railway, the Docklands Light, and North Greenwich underground station - the largest in Europe - which connects with central London.

RIVERSIDE PUBLIC HOUSES

There are quite a few pubs in the docklands area that still retain some of the original atmosphere, and here are a few to whet your whistle.

TOWN OF RAMSGATE
62 Wapping High St. E1. A dimly lit pub where the *Hanging Judge* Jefferies finally got his due. The cellars were dungeons where convicts were kept prior to deportation to Australia.

CAPTAIN KIDD
108 Wapping High St. E1.
Not an old pub, but you would never know. Close by the police station and with a restaurant.

PROSPECT OF WHITBY
57 Wapping Wall, E1.
The oldest of all the riverside London pubs dating from 1520. Samuel Pepys and Charles Dickens drank here.

THE
PROSPECT OF WHITBY

THE GUN, 27 Cold Harbour, E14.
Across from the millennium dome, near the entrance to West India dock, it is alleged to be the place where Nelson brought Lady Hamilton; he lived nearby.

THE GUN

THE MAYFLOWER, 117 Rotherhithe St, SE16.
The Pilgrim Fathers ship was moored here and the ship's captain is buried across the street in St.Mary's.

THE ANGEL, 101 Bermondsey Wall East, SE16.
Parts of this pub are very ancient indeed. It also has very good views up river to Tower Bridge.

O₂ ARENA - MILLENNIUM DOME
Built to protect exhibition pavilions from the elements for the year-long show, this massive big top was built to last much longer than the celebrations. Designed by Richard Rogers, it is the same height as Nelson's Column and could encompass thirteen Albert Halls or two Wembley Stadiums, It is now used for concerts,etc. During 2012 it will be used for Olympic gymnastics.

INDEX TO STREETS

ABBREVIATIONS   *The letters following a name indicate the Square and Page Number*

App. - Approach	E. - East	Lit. - Little	Sth. - South
Arc. - Arcade	Emb. - Embankment	Lr. - Lower	Sq. - Square
Av. - Avenue	Est. - Estate	Ms. - Mews	Sta. - Station
Bri. - Bridge	Flds. - Fields	Mt. - Mount	St. - Street
Blds. - Buildings	Gdns.- Gardens	Nth. - North	Ter. - Terrace
Cir. - Circus	Gte. - Gate.	Pal. - Palace	Up. - Upper
Clo. - Close	Gt. - Great	Pde. - Parade	Vw. - View
Cotts.- Cottages	Grn. - Green	Pk. - Park	Vs. - Villas
Ct. - Court	Gro. - Grove	Pass.- Passage	Wk. - Walk
Cres. - Crescent	Ho. - House	Pl. - Place	W. - West
Dri. - Drive	La. - Lane	Rd. - Road	Yd. - Yard

PRINCESS DIANA MEMORIAL FOUNTAIN   B2 40

A

Abbey St.	H4 45
Abbey Orchard St.	D4 42
Abbots La.	H1 45
Abbotsbury Rd.	A2 38
Aberdeen Pl.	A6 24
Aberdour St.	G5 45
Abingdon Rd.	D4 38
Abingdon St.	E4 43
Abingdon Villas	D5 38
Acacia Rd.	B2 24
Acklam Rd.	B2 30
Acton St.	G4 27
Adams Row	G5 33
Adam St.	F5 35
Addington St.	G3 43
Addison Cres.	A4 38
Addison Rd.	B4 38
Adelaide Rd.	A4 23
Adeline Pl.	D2 34
Agdon St.	B5 28
Ainger Rd.	A5 46
Aintree St.	A5 23
Aisgill Av.	C2 46
Albany St.	H2 25
Albemarle St.	A6 34
Albert Bri.	D4 48
Albert Ct.	A3 40
Albert Emb.	F2 51
Albert Sq.	G6 51
Albert St.	A1 26
Albert Ter.	F1 25
Albert Ter. Mews	A6 23
Albert Bri. Rd.	D5 48
Albion St. W2	C4 32
Albion St. EC1	B1 36
Aldebert Ter.	F6 51
Aldermanbury	E3 37
Alderney St.	A1 50
Aldersgate St.	D1 36
Aldford St.	G6 33
Aldgate	B3 52
Aldgate High St.	C3 52
Aldwych	G4 35
Alexander Pl	C5 40
Alexander St.	E3 31
Alfred Pl.	C1 34
Alie St.	D3 52
Allcroft Rd.	B2 23
Allen St.	D4 38
Allen Edwards Dri.	E6 51
All Saints Rd.	B3 30
All Saints St.	F2 27
Allington St.	A4 42
Allitsen Rd.	B2 24
Allsop Pl.	E6 25
Alma Street	D3 23
Alpha Pl.	D3 48
Amberley Rd.	E1 31
Ambrosden Av.	B5 42
America St.	D1 44
Ampton St.	G4 27
Amwell St.	A4 28
Anderson St.	D1 48
Angel Passage	F5 37
Angel St.	D3 36
Anglers Lane	D3 23
Anhalt Rd.	D5 48
Ann La.	A4 48
Anselm Rd.	C4 46
Appold St.	G1 37
Archel Rd.	B3 46
Argyle Sq.	F4 27
Argyle St.	E4 27
Argyll Rd.	D3 38
Argyll St.	B4 34
Arlington Av. & Sq.	E1 29
Arlington Rd.	A1 26
Arlington St.	B1 42
Arlington Way	B4 28

Artesian Rd.	C4 30
Arthur St.	F5 37
Artillery Lane	C1 52
Artillery Row	C5 42
Arundel Gdns.	B4 30
Arundel St.	H4 35
Ascalon St.	B6 50
Ashbridge St.	C6 24
Ashburn Gdns.	G6 39
Ashburn Pl.	G6 39
Ashburnham Rd.	H5 47
Ashby St.	C4 28
Ashley Pl.	B5 42
Ashmill St.	C1 32
Astell St.	C2 48
Athlone St.	C2 23
Atterbury St.	E1 51
Attneave St.	H5 27
Aubrey Rd.	C1 38
Aubrey Walk	C1 38
Augustus St.	A3 26
Austin Friars	F3 37
Austral St.	B5 44
Ave Maria La.	C3 36
Avenue Rd.	C1 24
Avery Row	H4 33
Avonmore Rd.	B6 38
Aybrook St.	F2 33
Aylesbury St.	B6 28
Aylesford St.	C2 50
Ayres St.	E2 45

B

Back Hill	A6 28
Baker St.	F2 33
Balcombe St.	D1 32
Baldwin's Gdns.	H2 35
Balfe St.	F2 27
Balfour St.	E6 45
Baltic St.	D6 28
Bankside	C6 36
Banner St.	E6 29
Barclay Rd.	D6 46
Barford St.	B1 28
Baring St.	F1 29
Bark Pl.	F5 31
Barkston Gdns.	E1 47
Barnby St.	B3 26
Barnsbury Rd.	H2 27
Baron St.	A2 28
Baron's Ct. Rd.	A2 46
Barrow Hill Rd.	B3 24
Bartholomew St.	F5 45
Bartholomew Villas	D3 23
Basil St.	E3 41
Basinghall Av.	E2 37
Basinghall St.	E3 37
Bassett St.	B2 23
Bastwick St.	D5 28
Bateman St.	D4 34
Bateman's Row.	H5 29
Bath St..	E4 29
Bath Ter.	D4 44
Battersea Bri.	B5 48
Battersea Bri Rd.	C6 48
Battersea Ch. Rd.	B6 48
Battersea Pk. Rd.	A6 50
Battle Bri. La.	A6 52
Battle Bri Rd.	E2 27
Bayham St.	A1 26
Bayley St.	D2 34
Baylis Rd.	A3 44
Bayswater Rd.	B5 32
Beak St.	B5 34
Bear Gardens	D6 36
Bear La.	C1 44
Beauchamp Pl.	D4 40
Beaufort Gdns.	D4 40
Beaufort St.	A3 48
Beaumont Av.	B2 46

Beaumont Cres.	B2 46
Beaumont St.	G1 33
Bedale St.	F1 45
Bedford Av.	D2 34
Bedfordbury.	E5 35
Bedford Gdns.	D1 38
Bedford Pl.	E1 35
Bedford Row	G2 35
Bedford Sq.	D2 34
Bedford St.	E5 35
Bedford Way	D6 26
Beech St.	D1 36
Beeston Pl.	H4 41
Belgrave Mews West	F4 41
Belgrave Pl.	G4 41
Belgrave Rd.	B1 50
Belgrave Sq.	F4 41
Bell La.	C1 52
Bell St.	C1 32
Bell Yard	H3 35
Belmont St.	B4 23
Belvedere Rd.	G2 43
Bemerton St.	F1 27
Benjamin St.	B1 36
Bentinck St.	G3 33
Berkeley Gdns.	E1 39
Berkeley Sq.	H5 33
Berkeley St.	A6 34
Berkley Road	A5 23
Bermondsey St.	G2 45
Bernard St.	E6 27
Berners Rd.	B1 28
Berners St.	B2 34
Berwick St.	C3 34
Bessborough Gdns.	D2 50
Bessborough Pl.	D2 50
Bessborough St.	C2 50
Bevan St.	E1 29
Bevenden St.	F3 29
Bevington Rd.	A2 30
Bevis Marks	B2 52
Bickenhall St.	E1 33
Bidborough St.	E4 27
Billiter St.	B3 52
Bina Gdns	G1 47
Birdcage Walk	B3 42
Bishop's Rd.	B6 46
Bishop's Ter	A6 44
Bishop's Bri. Rd	F3 31
Bishopsgate	G3 37
Bishop King's Rd.	A6 38
Blackfriars Bri.	B5 36
Black Friars La.	C4 36
Blackfriars Rd.	B3 44
Black Prince Rd.	G1 51
Blagrove Rd.	A2 30
Blake Gdns.	E6 47
Blandford St.	E2 33
Blenheim Cres.	A4 30
Blomfield Rd.	F1 31
Blomfield St.	G2 37
Blomfield Vs.	G2 31
Bloomfield Ter.	G2 49
Bloom Park Rd.	B6 46
Bloomsbury Sq.	F2 35
Bloomsbury St.	D2 34
Bloomsbury Way	E2 35
Bolingbroke Wk.	B6 48
Bolney St.	F5 51
Bolsover St.	A1 34
Bolton Gdns.	F1 47
Boltons, The	G2 47
Bondway	F3 51
Bonnington Sq.	G3 51
Boot St.	G4 29
Borough Rd.	C4 44
Borough High St.	E3 45
Boscobel St.	B1 32
Boston Pl	D6 24
Boswell St.	F1 35

Botolph La.	G5 37
Bourdon St.	H5 33
Bourne St.	F1 49
Bourne Ter.	E2 31
Bouverie St.	A4 36
Bow St.	F4 35
Bowling Grn. La.	A6 28
Bowling Grn. St.	H3 51
Bowling Grn. Wk.	G4 29
Braham St.	D2 52
Bramber Rd.	B4 46
Bramerton St.	B3 48
Bramham Gdns.	F1 46
Brandon St	E6 45
Bread St.	E4 37
Breams Blds.	A3 36
Brechin Pl.	H1 47
Brecon Rd	A4 46
Bremner Rd.	H4 39
Bressenden Pl.	A4 42
Brewer St.	C5 34
Brick La.	D1 52
Brick St.	G2 41
Bridge St.	E3 43
Bridgefoot	F3 51
Bridgeman St.	B2 24
Bridle La.	C4 34
Bridport Pl.	F1 29
Britannia Rd.	E6 47
Britannia Row	D1 28
Britannia St.	F4 27
Britten St.	C2 48
Britton St.	B1 36
Brixton Rd.	H6 51
Broad Sanctuary	E3 43
Broadley St.	C1 32
Broadmead	A6 50
Broad Walk, The	F1 39
Broadway	C4 42
Broadwick St.	B4 34
Brockham St.	E4 45
Bromfield St.	B1 28
Brompton Rd.	C5 40
Brompton Sq.	C4 40
Brook Dri.	A5 44
Brook St.	G4 33
Brooke St.	A2 36
Brooksville Rd.	B6 46
Brown St.	D3 32
Brownlow St.	G2 35
Brunswick Gdns.	E1 39
Brunswick Pl.	F4 29
Brunswick Sq.	F5 27
Brushfield St.	B1 52
Bruton Pl.	H5 33
Bruton St.	H5 33
Bryanston Pl.	D2 32
Bryanston Sq.	E3 33
Bryanston St.	E4 33
Buck St.	D5 23
Buckingham Gate	A4 42
Buckingham Pal. Rd.	H6 41
Buckland St.	G2 29
Bulstrode St.	G2 33
Bunhill Row	E5 29
Burge St.	F4 45
Burgh St.	C2 28
Burghley Road	D1 23
Burlington Arcade	B6 34
Burlington Gdns.	B5 34
Burnaby St.	G6 47
Burnstall St.	C2 48
Burnthwaite Rd.	C6 46
Burrell St.	C1 44
Burton St.	D5 26
Burwood Pl.	C3 32
Bury Pl.	E2 35
Bury St. SW1	B6 34
Bury St. EC3	H3 37

Earlham St.	E4 35	Featherstone Rd.	F5 29	Goldington St.	C2 26
Earl's Ct. Gdns.	E1 47	Fenchurch St.	A3 52	Goldsboro. Rd.	D6 50
Earl's Ct. Rd.	E1 47	Fentiman Rd.	F4 51	Goodge St.	C2 34
Earl's Ct. Sq.	E2 47	Ferdinand St.	B4 23	Goodman's Stile	D2 52
Earsby St.	A5 38	Fernhurst Rd.	A6 46	Goodman's Yard	C4 52
East Rd.	F4 29	Fernshaw Rd.	G4 47	Goods Way	E2 27
Eastbourne Ter.	H3 31	Fetter Lane	A3 36	Gopsall St.	F1 29
Eastcastle St.	B3 34	Filmer Rd.	B6 46	Gordon Pl.	E2 39
East Smithfield	D5 52	Finborough Rd.	F3 47	Gordon Sq.	D6 26
Eaton Gate	F6 41	Finchley Rd.	A1 24	Gordon St.	C5 26
Eaton Pl.	F5 41	Finsbury Circus	F2 37	Gorleston St.	A6 38
Eaton Sq.	G5 41	Finsbury Pavement	F1 37	Goswell Rd.	B3 28
Eaton Ter.	F6 41	Finsbury Sq.	F1 37	Gough Pl.	A3 36
Ebbisham Dri.	G4 51	Finsbury St.	F1 37	Gough St.	G5 27
Ebury Bri.	G1 49	First St.	D5 40	Goulston St.	C2 52
Ebury Mews	G6 41	Fish St. Hill	G5 37	Gower Pl.	C5 26
Ebury Sq.	G1 49	Fitzalan St.	A6 44	Gower St.	C1 34
Ebury St.	G6 41	Fitz-George Av.	A6 38	Gracechurch St.	G4 37
Ebury Bri. Rd.	G2 49	Fitzjames Av.	A6 38	Grafton Cres.	D5 23
Eccleston Bri.	H6 41	Fitzroy Road	A6 23	Grafton Pl.	D4 26
Eccleston Pl.	H6 41	Fitzroy Sq.	B6 26	Grafton Rd.	B1 23
Eccleston Sq.	A6 42	Fitzroy St.	B1 34	Grafton St.	A5 34
Eccleston St.	G5 41	Flaxman Ter.	D5 26	Grafton Ter.	A2 23
Edgware Rd.	B1 32	Fleet St.	A4 36	Grafton Way	B6 26
Edith Gro.	G4 47	Flood St.	D3 48	Graham St.	C2 28
Edith Rd.	A1 46	Floral St.	E4 35	Graham Ter.	F1 49
Edith Ter.	G5 47	Foley St.	B2 34	Granary St.	C1 26
Edith Villas	E1 46	Folgate St.	H1 37	Granby Ter.	A3 26
Edis Street	B6 23	Fore St.	E2 37	Grange Rd.	H4 45
Edwardes Sq.	C5 38	Formosa St.	F1 31	Grange Walk	H4 45
Effie Rd.	D6 46	Forston Rd.	E2 29	Granville Sq.	H4 27
Egbert Street	B6 23	Fortes Road	D1 23	Gravel La.	C2 52
Egerton Cres.	C5 40	Fortune St.	E6 29	Gray St.	B3 44
Egerton Gdns.	C5 40	Foster Lane	D3 36	Gray's Inn Rd.	F4 27
Egerton Ter.	C5 40	Foulis Ter.	A1 48	Gt. Castle St.	A3 34
Elcho St.	C6 48	Fount St.	D6 50	Gt. Chapel St.	C3 34
Eldon Rd.	F4 39	Frampton St.	A6 24	Gt. College St.	E4 43
Eldon St.	G2 37	Francis St.	B5 42	Gt. Cumberland Pl.	E3 33
Elephant Rd.	D5 44	Franklin's Row	E2 49	Gt. Dover St.	F4 45
Elgin Cres.	A5 30	Frazier St.	A3 44	Gt. Eastern St.	G5 29
Elia St.	C3 28	Frederick St.	G4 27	Gt. George St.	D3 42
Elizabeth Bri.	H6 41	Friday St.	D4 36	Gt. Guildford St.	D1 44
Elizabeth St.	G6 41	Friend St.	B3 28	Gt. James St.	G1 35
Elkstone Rd.	B1 30	Frith St.	C4 34	Gt. Marlborough St.	B4 34
Elliot's Row	C5 44	Frome St.	D2 28	Gt. Ormond St.	F1 35
Ellis St.	E6 41	Fulham Broadway	D5 46	Gt. Percy St.	G4 27
Elm St.	H6 27	Fulham Rd.	F5 47	Gt. Peter St.	D5 42
Elm Park Gdns.	A3 48	Furnival St.	A3 36	Gt. Portland St.	A1 34
Elm Park Rd.	A3 48			Gt. Queen St.	F3 35
Elm Tree Rd.	A3 24	**G**		Gt. Russell St.	D2 34
Elvaston Pl.	G4 39	Gambia St.	C2 44	Gt. Scotland Yd.	E1 43
Elverton St.	C5 42	Ganton St.	B4 34	Gt. Smith St.	D4 42
Elystan Pl.	D1 48	Garden Row	C4 44	Gt. Suffolk St.	C2 44
Elystan St.	C1 48	Garway Rd.	E4 31	Gt. Sutton St.	C6 28
Embankment Gdns.	E3 49	Gaskin St.	C1 28	Gt. Titchfield St.	A1 34
Emerson St.	D6 36	Gateforth St.	B6 24	Gt. Tower St.	A4 52
Emery Hill St.	C5 42	Gatliff Rd.	G2 49	Gt. Western Rd.	C1 30
Emperor's Gate	F5 39	Gayfere St.	E5 43	Gt. Windmill St.	C5 34
Endell St.	E3 35	Gaywood St.	C5 44	Greek St.	D4 34
Endsleigh Gdns.	C5 26	George St.	D3 32	Greenberry St.	C3 24
Endsleigh Pl.	D5 26	Gerald St.	G6 41	Greencoat Pl.	C5 42
Endsleigh St.	D5 26	Geraldine St.	B5 44	Green St.	F4 33
Enford St.	D1 32	Gerrard Rd.	C2 28	Greenwell St.	A1 34
Ennismore Gdns.	C3 40	Gerrard St.	D4 34	Greenwood Pl.	D1 23
Ennismore Gdns. Ms.	C4 40	Gerridge St.	A4 44	Greet St.	B2 44
Ennismore St.	C4 40	Gertrude St.	H4 47	Grenville Pl.	G5 37
Epworth St.	F6 29	Gilbert Rd.	B6 44	Grenville St. WC1	F6 27
Erasmus St.	D1 50	Gilbert St.	G4 33	Gresham St.	E3 37
Erskine Rd.	A5 23	Gilden St.	B1 23	Gresse St.	C2 34
Escourt Rd.	A5 46	Gillies St.	C2 23	Greville St. EC1	A2 36
Essex Rd.	C1 28	Gillingham St.	A6 42	Greycoat Pl.	C5 42
Essex St.	H4 35	Gilston Rd.	H3 47	Greycoat St.	C5 42
Essex Villas	D3 38	Giltspur St.	C3 36	Greyhound Rd.	A3 46
Eton Road	A4 23	Gironde Rd.	C6 46	Grosvenor Cres.	F3 41
Eton College Rd.	A4 23	Gladstone St.	B4 44	Grosvenor Gdns.	H4 41
Euston Rd.	A6 26	Glasshouse St	B5 34	Grosvenor Pl.	G3 41
Euston Sq.	C4 26	Glasshouse Wk.	F2 51	Grosvenor Rd.	B3 50
Euston St.	B5 26	Glazbury Rd.	A1 46	Grosvenor Sq.	G5 33
Evelyn Gdns.	H2 47	Glebe Pl.	C3 48	Grosvenor St.	G5 33
Evelyn Walk.	F3 29	Gledhow Gdns.	G1 47	Grove End Rd.	A3 24
Eversholt St.	B2 26	Gledstanes Rd.	A2 46	Guildford Rd.	E6 51
Ewer St.	D1 44	Globe St.	E4 45	Guildhouse St.	A6 42
Exhibition Rd.	B4 40	Gloucester Av.	A5 23	Guilford St.	F6 27
Exmouth Market	A5 28	Gloucester Cres.	C6 23	Gunter Gro.	G4 47
Exton St.	A2 44	Gloucester Gate	C2 25	Gunterstone Rd.	A1 46
		Gloucester Pl.	E1 33	Gutter Lane	D3 36
F		Gloucester Rd.	G4 39	Guy St.	F3 45
Fabian Rd.	C5 46	Gloucester Sq.	B4 32	Gwendwr Rd.	A1 46
Falkirk St.	H3 29	Gloucester St.	A2 50		
Falmouth Rd.	E5 45	Gloucester Ter.	G3 31	**H**	
Fann St.	D6 28	Gloucester Way	B4 28	Haberdasher St.	F4 29
Fanshaw St.	G3 29	Glyn St.	F3 51	Hackford Rd.	H6 51
Farm La.	D5 46	Godfrey St.	C2 48	Hackney Rd.	H4 29
Farm St.	G6 33	Goding St.	F2 51	Hadley St.	C3 23
Farrier St.	D4 23	Godliman St.	D4 36	Haldane Rd.	C5 46
Farringdon Rd.	A5 28	Golbourne Rd.	A2 30	Half Moon Cres.	H2 27
Farringdon St.	B3 36	Golden La.	D6 28	Half Moon St.	H1 41
Fashion St.	C1 52	Golden Sq.	B5 34	Halford Rd.	D4 46
Fawcett St.	G4 47	Goldington Cres.	C2 26	Halkin Arcade	F4 41

Halkin St.	G3 41
Hall Pl.	A6 24
Hall Rd.	A4 24
Hall St.	C3 28
Hallam St.	A1 34
Halsey St.	D6 40
Hamilton Pl.	G2 41
Hamilton Ter.	A5 24
Hammersmith Rd.	A5 38
Hampstead Rd.	B3 26
Hampton St.	D6 44
Handel St.	E5 27
Handforth Rd.	H5 51
Hannell Rd.	A5 46
Hanover Gate	C4 24
Hanover Gdns.	H4 51
Hanover Sq.	A4 34
Hans Cres.	D4 40
Hans Pl.	E4 41
Hans Rd.	D4 40
Harbet Rd.	B2 32
Harcourt St.	D2 32
Harcourt Ter.	F3 47
Hardwick St.	A4 28
Harewood Av.	D1 32
Harewood Pl.	A4 34
Harewood Row	D1 32
Harley Gdns.	H2 47
Harley St.	G1 33
Harleyford Rd.	G3 51
Harleyford St	H4 51
Harmood St.	C4 23
Harper Rd	D4 44
Harpur St.	F1 35
Harrington Gdns.	G6 39
Harrington Rd.	A6 40
Harrington Sq.	B2 26
Harrison St.	F4 27
Harrow Pl.	B2 52
Harrow Rd.	D1 30
Harrowby St.	D3 32
Hart St.	B4 52
Hartington Rd.	E6 51
Hartismere Rd.	C5 46
Hartland Rd.	C4 23
Harwood Rd.	E6 47
Hasker St.	D5 40
Hastings St	E4 27
Hatfields	B1 44
Hatton Garden	A1 36
Hatton Wall	A1 36
Havelock St.	F1 27
Havelock Ter.	A6 50
Haverstock Hill	A3 23
Haverstock Rd.	A1 23
Hawley Cres.	D5 23
Hawley Rd.	D4 23
Hawley St.	C5 23
Hay Hill	A6 34
Hayes Pl.	D1 32
Hayles St.	B5 44
Haymarket	D6 34
Hays La.	G1 45
Hays Mews	H6 33
Headfort Pl.	G3 41
Heathcote St.	F5 27
Helmet Row	D5 28
Hemingford Rd.	H1 27
Hemsworth St.	G2 29
Henrietta Pl.	H3 33
Henrietta St.	E5 35
Henshaw St.	F6 45
Herbal Hill	A6 28
Herbert St.	A2 23
Herbrand St.	E6 27
Hercules Rd.	H4 43
Hereford Rd.	D3 30
Hereford Sq.	H6 39
Heriot Place	A1 23
Herrick St.	D1 50
Hertford St.	H1 41
Hester Rd.	C5 48
Heygate St.	F5 51
Heygate St.	D6 44
Hide Pl.	C6 42
Highgate Rd.	D1 23
High Holborn	F2 35
Hildyard Rd.	D4 46
Hill St.	G6 33
Hillgate St.	D1 38
Hillsleigh Rd.	C1 38
Hinde St.	G3 33
Hobart Pl.	G4 41
Hobury St.	H4 47
Hogarth Rd.	E6 39
Holbein Place	F1 49
Holborn	H2 35
Holborn Circus	A2 36
Holborn Viaduct	B2 36

Holland Park	B2 38
Holland Rd.	A4 38
Holland St. SE1	C1 44
Holland St. W8	D3 38
Holland Pk. Av.	A2 38
Holland Pk. Gdns.	A2 38
Holland Pk. Rd.	B4 38
Holland Villas Rd.	A3 38
Holles St.	H3 33
Hollywood Rd.	G3 47
Holmead Rd.	F5 47
Holmes Rd.	D2 23
Holyoake Rd.	C6 44
Holywell La.	H5 29
Homer St.	D2 32
Homestead Rd.	B5 46
Hopton St.	C1 44
Horbury Cres.	C6 30
Hormead Rd.	B1 30
Hornton St.	D2 38
Horseferry Rd.	D5 42
Horse Guards Av.	E1 43
Horse Guards Rd.	D2 42
Horselydown La.	C6 52
Hortensia Rd.	G5 47
Howick Pl.	B5 42
Howie St	C6 48
Howland St.	B1 34
Howley Pl.	H1 31
Hoxton Sq.	H4 29
Hoxton St.	H2 29
Hugh St.	A6 42
Humbolt Rd.	A4 46
Hungerford Footbridge	F1 43
Hunter St.	E5 27
Huntley St.	C1 34
Hyde Rd.	G1 29
Hyde Pk. Corner	G2 41
Hyde Pk. Cres	C3 32
Hyde Pk. Gate	H3 39
Hyde Pk. Gdns	B4 32
Hyde Pk. Sq.	C4 32
Hyde Pk. St.	C4 32

I

Ifield Rd.	F3 47
Ilchester Gardens	E5 31
Ilchester Pl.	B4 38
Inglebert St.	A3 28
Inkerman Rd.	D2 23
Inner Circle	F4 25
Inverness St.	C6 23
Inverness Ter.	F4 31
Ironmonger Row	D4 28
Irving St.	D5 34
Islington High St.	B2 28
Ives St.	C6 40
Ivor Pl.	D6 24
Ivy St.	G2 29
Ixworth Pl.	C1 48

J

James St. W1	G3 33
James St. WC2	E4 35
Jamestown Rd.	C6 23
Jeffrey's St.	D4 23
Jerdan Pl.	D5 46
Jermyn St.	B6 34
Jewry St.	C3 52
Joan St.	B2 44
Jockey's Fields	G1 35
John St.	G1 35
John Adam St.	F6 35
John Islip St.	D1 50
Johnson's Pl.	B2 50
Jonathan St.	G1 51
Jubilee Pl.	D2 48
Judd St.	E4 27
Juer St.	C3 48
Juxon St.	G5 43

K

Kelly Street	D3 23
Kelvedon Rd.	C6 46
Kemble St.	F4 35
Kempsford Gdns.	E2 47
Kempson Rd.	E6 47
Kendal St.	C4 32
Kennington La.	G2 51
Kennington Oval	H4 51
Kennington Rd.	A4 44
Kensington Ct.	F3 39
Kensington Gore	A3 40
Kensington Pl.	D1 38
Kensington Rd.	F3 39
Kensington Sq.	F3 39
Kensington Ch. St.	D1 38
Kensington Ct. Pl.	F4 39

Kensington Gdns. Sq.	E4 31
Kensington High St.	B5 38
Kensington Pal.Gdns.	E6 31
Kensington Pk. Gdns.	B5 30
Kensington Pk. Rd.	B4 30
Kentish Town Rd.	D5 23
Kenton St.	E5 27
Kenway Rd.	E6 39
Keppell St.	D1 34
Keyworth St.	C4 44
Kildare Gdns.	E3 31
Kildare Ter.	E3 31
Killick St.	G2 27
Kilmaine Rd	A6 46
King St. EC2	E3 37
King St. SW1	B1 42
King St. WC2	E5 35
King Charles St.	E2 43
King Edward St.	D3 36
King Edward Walk	A4 44
King Henry's Rd.	A5 23
Kingly St.	B4 34
King's Boulevard	E2 27
King's Rd.	B3 48
King's Cross Rd.	G3 27
Kingsland Rd.	H3 29
Kingsway	F3 35
King William St.	F4 37
Kirby St.	A1 36
Kirtling St.	B5 50
Knaresboro Pl.	E6 39
Knightsbridge	D3 40
Kipling St.	F3 45
Kynance Ms.	F5 39

L

Ladbroke Gdns.	B5 30
Ladbroke Gro.	A3 30
Ladbroke Rd.	B6 30
Ladbroke Sq.	C6 30
Ladbroke Ter.	C6 30
Lambeth Bri.	F5 43
Lambeth High St.	F6 43
Lambeth Rd.	G5 43
Lambeth Walk	H5 43
Lambeth Pal. Rd.	F5 43
Lamb St.	A1 23
Lamb's Conduit St.	G1 35
Lamont Rd.	H4 47
Lancaster Gate	H5 31
Lancaster Pl.	G5 35
Lancaster Rd.	A3 30
Lancaster St.	C3 44
Lancaster Ter.	A5 32
Lancelot Pl.	D3 40
Langham St.	A2 34
Langham St.	A2 34
Langley La.	F3 51
Langton St.	H4 47
Lansdowne Cres.	A5 30
Lansdowne Gdns.	E6 51
Lansdowne Rise	A5 30
Lansdowne Rd.	A5 30
Lansdowne Ter.	F6 27
Lansdowne Wk.	B6 30
Lant St.	D3 44
Launceston Pl.	G4 39
Lavington St.	C1 44
Law St.	F4 45
Lawn La.	F4 51
Lawrence St.	C4 48
Laystall St.	H6 27
Leadenhall St.	A3 52
Leamington Rd. Vs.	C2 30
Leather Lane	A1 36
Leathermarket St.	G3 45
Ledbury Rd.	C3 30
Lees Place	F5 33
Leicester Sq.	D5 34
Leigh St.	E5 27
Leinster Gdns.	G4 31
Leinster Pl.	G4 31
Leinster Sq.	E4 31
Leinster Ter.	G5 31
Leman St.	D3 52
Lennox Gdns.	D5 40
Leonard St.	F5 29
Leroy St.	G5 45
Lever St.	D4 28
Lexham Gdns.	E5 39
Lexington St.	C4 34
Leybourne Rd.	C4 23
Liberty St.	H6 51
Library St.	C3 44
Lidlington Pl.	B3 26
Lilestone St.	C6 24
Lillie Rd.	A4 46
Lilyville Rd	B6 46

Lime St.	G4 37
Limerston St.	H3 47
Lincoln's Inn Fields	G3 35
Linden Gdns.	D6 30
Linton St.	E1 29
Lisgar Ter.	B6 38
Lisle St.	D5 34
Lisson Grove	B5 24
Lisson St.	C1 32
Little Boltons, The	F2 47
Little Britain	D2 36
Little College St.	F4 43
Little Dorrit Ct.	E2 45
Liverpool Rd.	A2 28
Liverpool St.	G2 37
Lloyd Sq.	H4 27
Lloyd St.	H4 27
Lloyd Baker St.	H4 27
Lloyd's Av.	B3 52
Lodge Rd.	B5 24
Logan Pl.	D6 38
Lollard St.	H6 43
Loman St.	C2 44
Lombard St.	F4 37
London Bri.	F6 37
London Rd.	C4 44
London St.	A3 32
London Wall	E2 37
London Bri. St.	F1 45
Long Acre	E4 35
Long La. EC1	C2 36
Long La. SE1	F3 45
Longford St.	A5 26
Longmoore St.	B6 42
Longridge Rd.	D6 38
Lonsdale Rd.	B4 30
Lord North St.	E5 43
Lorenzo St.	G3 27
Lothbury	F3 37
Lots Rd.	G6 47
Loudoun Rd	A2 24
Loughborough St.	H2 51
Love La.	E3 37
Lr. Belgrave St.	H5 41
Lr Grosvenor Pl.	H4 41
Lower Marsh	H3 43
Lr. Regent St.	C6 34
Lr. Sloane St.	F1 49
Lr. Thames St.	G5 37
Lowndes Pl.	F4 41
Lowndes Sq.	E3 41
Lowndes St.	E4 41
Lucan Pl.	C6 40
Ludgate Circus	B4 36
Ludgate Hill	C4 36
Luke St.	G5 29
Lupus St.	A2 50
Lurline Gdns.	G6 49
Luxborough St.	F1 33
Lyall St.	F5 41

M

Mabledon Pl.	D4 26
Macclesfield Bri.	D2 24
Macclesfield Rd.	D4 28
Maclise Rd.	A5 38
Maddox St.	A4 34
Magdalen St.	H2 45
Maida Av.	H1 31
Maida Vale	A6 24
Maiden La.	E5 35
Maitland Park Rd.	A3 23
Maitland Pk. Villas	A2 23
Malden Cres.	B4 23
Malden Rd.	B3 23
Malet St.	D1 34
Mall, The	C2 42
Mallord St.	B3 48
Manchester Sq.	F3 33
Manchester St.	F2 33
Manciple St.	F3 45
Mandeville Pl.	G3 33
Manresa Rd.	B2 48
Mansell St.	C3 52
Mansfield St.	H2 33
Mansfield Rd.	A1 23
Maple St.	B1 34
Marble Arch	E4 33
Marchmont St.	E5 27
Margaret St.	A3 34
Mark La.	B4 52
Market Pl.	B3 34
Markham Square	D2 48
Markham St.	D2 48
Marlborough Pl.	A2 24
Marloes Rd.	E5 39
Marsden St.	B3 23
Marshall St.	B4 34

Marshalsea Rd.	D2 44
Marsham St.	D5 42
Martin Lane	F5 37
Marville Rd.	B6 46
Mary St.	E1 29
Marylands Rd.	D1 30
Marylebone La.	G3 33
Marylebone Rd.	C1 32
Marylebone High St.	G2 33
Mason St.	G6 45
Massinger St.	G6 45
Matheson Rd.	B1 46
Matilda St.	G1 27
Mawbey St.	E6 51
Maxwell Rd.	F6 47
Maygood St.	H2 27
Meadow Row	D5 44
Meadow Rd.	G5 51
Mecklenburgh Pl.	G6 27
Mecklenburgh Sq.	G5 27
Medway St.	D5 42
Melbury Ct.	C4 38
Melbury Rd.	C4 38
Melcombe Pl.	D1 32
Melcombe St.	E1 33
Melton St.	C5 26
Mendora Rd.	A5 46
Mercer St.	E4 35
Meredith St.	B4 28
Merrington Rd.	D3 46
Meymott St.	B1 44
Micawber St.	C3 28
Michael Rd.	F6 47
Micklethwaite Rd.	D4 46
Middlesex St.	B1 52
Midland Rd.	D3 26
Milborne Gro.	H3 47
Miles St.	E4 51
Milk St.	E3 37
Milford Lane	H4 35
Mill St.	A4 34
Millbank	E5 43
Millman St.	G6 27
Milman's St.	A4 48
Milner St.	D6 40
Milton Ct.	E1 37
Milton St.	E1 37
Mincing La.	B4 52
Minories	C3 52
Mintern St.	F2 29
Mirabel Rd.	B5 46
Mitchell St.	D5 28
Mitre Rd.	B2 44
Mitre St.	B3 52
Monck St.	D5 42
Monkton St.	B6 44
Monmouth St.	E4 35
Montagu Pl. W1	E2 33
Montagu Sq.	E2 33
Montagu St. W1	E3 33
Montague Clo.	F6 37
Montague Pl. WC1	D2 34
Montague St. WC1	E2 35
Montford Pl.	H3 51
Montpelier Pl.	C4 40
Montpelier Sq.	C3 40
Montpelier St.	D4 40
Montpelier Wk.	C4 40
Montrose Pl.	G3 41
Monument St.	G5 37
Moor La.	E2 37
Moore St.	D6 40
Moorfields	F2 37
Moorgate	F3 37
Moorhouse Rd.	D3 30
Moor Pk. Rd.	E6 47
Mora St.	E4 29
Morat St.	H6 51
Moreland St.	C4 28
Moreton Pl.	B1 50
Moreton St.	C2 50
Morgan's La.	B6 52
Morley St.	A3 44
Mornington Av.	B1 46
Mornington Cres.	A2 26
Mornington St.	A2 26
Mornington Ter.	A2 26
Morocco St.	G3 45
Morpeth Ter.	B5 42
Mortimer St.	B2 34
Moscow Rd.	E5 31
Mossop St.	D6 40
Motcomb St.	F4 41
Mount Row	G5 33
Mount St.	F6 33
Mt. Pleasant	H6 27
Moylan Rd.	A4 46
Mulberry Walk	B3 48
Mulgrave Rd.	B4 46

Welbeck St.	G2 33	Weston St.	G2 45	Wilfred St.	B4 42	Woodfield Rd.	C1 30
Wellesley Rd.	B2 23	West Smithfield	C2 36	Wilkin St.	C3 23	Wooton St.	A2 44
Wellesley Ter.	E3 29	Westway	B2 30	Wilkinson St.	F6 51	Worfield St.	D6 47
Wellington Pl.	B3 24	Wetherby Gdns.	G1 47	Willes Rd.	C2 23	Wormwood St.	G3 37
Wellington Rd.	B3 24	Wetherby Pl.	G6 39	William Rd.	B5 26	Wornington Rd.	A1 30
Wellington Sq.	D2 48	Weymouth St.	G2 33	William St.	E3 41	Woronzow Rd.	B1 24
Wellington St.	F4 35	Wharf Rd.	D2 28	William IV St.	E5 35	Worship St.	G6 29
Wells Rise	D1 24	Wharfedale Rd.	F2 27	Willow Pl.	B6 42	Wren St.	G5 27
Wells St.	B2 34	Wharton St.	H4 27	Willow Wk.	H5 45	Wright's La.	E4 39
Wenlock Rd.	D3 28	Whitcomb St.	D6 34	Wilmington Sq.	A5 28	Wyclif St.	B4 28
Wenlock St.	E3 29	Whitechapel High St.	C2 52	Wilmington St.	A4 28	Wyfold Rd.	A6 46
Wentworth St.	C1 52	Whitecross St.	E6 29	Wilton Cres.	F3 41	Wyndham Pl.	D2 32
Werrinton St.	C3 26	Whitefriars St.	B2 36	Wilton Pl.	F3 41	Wynford Rd.	G2 27
West Sq.	B5 44	Whitehall	E2 43	Wilton Rd.	A5 42	Wynham St.	D1 32
West St.	D4 34	Whitehall Ct.	E1 43	Wilton Row	F3 41	Wynyatt St.	B4 28
Westbourne Gdns.	E3 31	Whitehall Pl.	E1 43	Wilton St.	G4 41	Wyvil St.	E5 51
Westbourne Gro.	C4 30	Whiteheads Gro.	D1 48	Wilton Ter.	F4 41		
Westbourne St.	A4 32	White Horse St.	H1 41	Wimbourne St.	E2 29	**Y**	
Westbourne Ter.	G2 31	White Kennett St.	B2 52	Wimpole St.	G2 33	Yardley St.	A5 28
Westbourne Pk. Rd.	C3 30	White Lion St.	A2 28	Winchester St	A2 50	Yeoman's Row	C5 40
Westbourne Pk. Vs.	E2 31	White's Grounds	H3 45	Wincott St.	A6 44	York Bri.	F5 25
Westbourne Ter. Rd.	G2 31	White's Row	C1 52	Windmill St.	C2 34	York Gate	F6 25
Westbridge Rd.	C6 48	Whitfield St.	B1 34	Windsor Ter.	E3 29	York Mews	D2 23
W. Cromwell Rd.	B1 46	Whitgift St.	G6 43	Winsland St.	A3 32	York Rd.	G3 43
W. Eaton Pl.	F5 41	Whitmore Rd.	G1 29	Woburn Pl.	E6 27	York St.	D2 32
Westgate Ter.	F3 47	Wichendon Rd.	B6 46	Woburn St.	D6 26	York Way	F1 27
West Halkin St.	F4 41	Wickham St.	G2 51	Woburn Wk.	D5 26	Young St.	F3 39
Westminster Bri.	F3 43	Wigmore St.	F3 33	Wood La.	E3 37		
Westminster Bri. Rd.	A4 44	Wilbraham Pl.	E6 41	Wood Mews	F5 33		
Westmoreland St.	G2 33	Wilcox Rd.	E5 51	Wood St.	E2 37		
Westmoreland Ter.	H2 49	Wild St.	F3 35	Woodbridge St.	B5 28		
Weston Rise	G3 27	Wilds Rents	G4 45				

HAMPSTEAD AND HIGHGATE INDEX
PAGES 56 - 57

Agincourt Rd.	A5 57	East Heath Rd.	C4 56	Keats Grove	D5 56	Pond Street	D6 56
Akenside Rd.	C6 56	Eldon Grove	D6 56	Kemplay Road	C5 56	Prince Arthur Rd.	B5 56
Alvanley Gdns.	A6 56	Ellerdale Rd.	B5 56	Kidderpore Av.	A5 56	Raydon Street	H3 57
Archway	H1 57	Estelle Road	F5 57	Kidderpore Gdns.	A5 56	Redington Rd.	A4 56
Arkwright Rd.	B6 56	Fawley Road	A6 56	Lady Somerset Rd.	H5 57	Robin Grove	G2 57
Belsize Av.	D6 56	Ferncroft Av.	A4 56	Langbourne Av.	G3 57	Roderick Rd.	F5 57
Belsize Cres.	D6 56	Finchley Road	A6 56	Langland Gdns.	B6 56	Rona Rd.	F5 57
Belsize La.	D6 56	Fitzjohn's Av.	C6 56	Laurier Rd.	H4 57	Rosecroft Av.	A4 56
Bishop's Av. The	D1 56	Fitzroy Park	F2 57	Lawn Road	E6 57	Rosslyn Hill	D5 56
Bishopswood Road	F1 57	Flask Walk	C5 56	Lindfield Gdns.	B6 56	Rudall Cres.	C5 56
Bracknell Gdns.	A5 56	Fleet Road	A5 57	Lisburne Road	F5 57	St. Albans Rd.	G4 57
Branch Hill	B4 56	Frognal	B5 56	Lissenden Gdns.	G5 57	Savernake Rd.	F5 57
Bromwich Av.	G3 57	Frognal Gdns.	B5 56	Lower Terrace	B4 56	Sheldon Av.	E1 57
Brookfield Park	H3 57	Frognal Lane	A6 56	Lymington Road	B6 56	Shirlock Rd.	F5 57
Burghley Road	H5 57	Garnett Road	E6 57	Lyndhurst Gdns.	D6 56	South Grove	G1 57
Cannon Hill	A6 56	Gayton Road	C5 56	Lyndhurst Rd.	C6 56	South End Rd.	D5 56
Cannon Lane	C4 56	Glenhurst Av.	G5 57	Lyndhurst Ter.	C6 56	South Hill Park	E5 57
Cannon Place	C4 56	Glenloch Road	E6 57	Mackeson Rd.	F5 57	Southwood Lane	G1 57
Carlingford Rd.	D5 56	Gordon House Rd.	G5 57	Makepeace Av.	G3 57	Spaniards Close	C1 56
Causton Rd.	H1 57	Greenaway Gdns.	A5 56	Merton Lane	F2 57	Spaniards Rd.	C3 56
Chandos Way	A1 56	Grove. The	G1 57	Millfield Lane	F3 57	Spencer Rise	H4 57
Chester Rd.	H3 57	Hampstead Grove	B4 56	Millfield Place	F3 57	Squire's Mount	C4 56
Chesterford Gdns.	B5 56	Hampstead Lane	E1 57	Mount Vernon	B5 56	Stormont Road	E1 57
Chetwynd Road	H4 57	Hampstead Way	A1 56	Nassington Rd.	E5 57	Streatley Place	C5 56
Cholmeley Cres.	H1 57	Hampstead High St.	C5 56	Netherhall Gdns.	C6 56	Swains Lane	G3 57
Cholmeley Park	H1 57	Hampstead Hill Gdns.	D5 56	Netherhall Way	B6 56	Tasker Road	F6 57
Christchurch Hill	C4 56	Haverstock Hill	E6 57	New End	C4 56	Tazna Road	E4 57
Church Row	B5 56	Heath Drive	A5 56	New End Square	C4 56	Templewood Av.	A4 56
Churchill Road	H4 57	Heath Street	C4 56	North End	B2 56	Thurlow Rd.	C6 56
Compton Av.	E1 57	Heath Hurst Rd.	D5 56	North Road	G1 57	Upper Terrace	B4 56
Constantine Road	A5 57	Highgate Hill	H2 57	North End Av.	B2 56	Upper Park Rd.	E6 57
Courthope Road	F5 57	Highgate Road	G4 57	North End Rd.	A1 56	Wedderburn Lane	D6 56
Crediton Hill	A6 56	Highgate High St.	G1 57	North End Way	B2 56	Well Road	C4 56
Cressy Road	E5 57	Highgate West Hill	G1 57	Oakeshot Av.	G3 57	Well Walk	C4 56
Croft Way	A5 56	Hillway	G3 57	Oakhill Av.	A5 56	Wellesley Road	G6 57
Croftdown Rd.	G4 57	Holford Road	C4 56	Oak Hill Way	B4 56	Wellgarth Rd.	A1 56
Cromwell Av.	H1 57	Holly Hill	B4 56	Oak Village	G5 57	West End Lane	A6 56
Daleham Gdns.	C6 56	Holly Walk	B5 56	Ornan Road	D6 56	West Heath Av.	A1 56
Dartmouth Park Hill	H2 57	Holly Lodge Gdns.	G2 57	Park. The	A2 56	West Heath Rd.	A3 56
Dartmouth Park Rd.	H4 57	Hollycroft Av.	A4 56	Park Av.	A2 56	Wildwood Rd.	B1 56
Denning Road	D5 56	Honeybourne Rd.	A6 56	Park Drive	A2 56	Willoughby Rd.	C5 56
Downshire Hill	D5 56	Hornsey Lane	H1 57	Parkhill Rd.	F6 57	Willow Road	C5 56
Downside Cres.	E6 57	Ingram Avenue	C1 56	Parliament Hill	A5 57	Windmill Hill	B4 56
				Perceval Av.	D6 56	Winnington Rd.	C1 56
				Pilgrim's Lane	D5 56	Woodsome Rd.	G4 57
				Platt's Lane	A3 56	York Rise	H4 57

Every effort has been made throughout this Mapguide to ensure that the information given is accurate, while the Publishers would be grateful to learn of errors, they can not accept responsibility for any loss or expense caused by any errors or updating which may have occurred.

I would like to thank British Waterways for permission to use their photograph of Snowdon's Aviary on page 58, and English Heritage for the Page 5 reproduction of 'Old London Bridge' by Claude de Jongh.
The Front Cover and Page I & 22 & 55 llustrations were by Ronald Maddox PRI, FCSD.
Page 33 'Laughing Cavalier' by kind permission of the Trustees of the Wallace Collection
The back cover photograph of the 'Achilles in Hyde Park' by Michael Middleditch
Page 23 Roundhouse at Twilight photograph by Gareth Gardner permission of the Roundhouse
Page 10 Noel Coward illustration by permission of the National Portrait Gallery,London
Globe theatre photograph page 12 by Richard Kalina permission of Shakespeare's Globe.
Inside Cover 'Balloon View of London' by permission of the British Library
30 St. Mary Axe on page 37 reproduced by permission of Swiss Re.
Page 55 Rainbow Portrait of Queen Elizabeth I by kind permission of The Marquess of Salisbury.
Page 55 Great Hall photograph by permission of Knebworth House.

MAPGUIDES & MAPS BY MICHAEL MIDDLEDITCH
PUBLISHED BY PENGUIN BOOKS

The PARIS MAPGUIDE   ISBN 9780 1414 69041
A 64-page double award-winning publication. Clear and colourful, containing a wealth of information including an original Metro map: easy to read and ideal to carry with you. Features on the Louvre, Versailles etc.

The NEW YORK MAPGUIDE   ISBN 9780 1402 94590
The indispensable guide to Manhattan, containing maps, entertainments, walks, a guide to the great 20th century architecture, as well as detailed plans of the Bronx Zoo, the Botanical Gardens and Prospect Park, Brooklyn.

The Penguin Map of THE WORLD   ISBN 9780 1405 15282
A clear, colourful map, crammed with information on an unusual projection. Ideal as a wall map for office or home. Features Flags of the World.

The ST. ALBANS MAPGUIDE   ISBN 9780 9513 39015
Published by MICHAEL GRAHAM PUBLICATIONS, This is the author's home town; it contains an ancient abbey, and the remains of Verulamium, the Roman town. The ST ALBANS MAPGUIDE won a British Cartographic Society award.

PENGUIN BOOKS
Published by the Penguin Group
Special Edition Published 2012
2 3 4 5 6 7 8 9 10
Penguin Books Ltd, 80 Strand, London WC2R 0RL, England
Penguin Group (USA) Inc., 375 Hudson Street, New York, New York 10014, USA
Penguin Group (Australia), 250 Camberwell Road, Camberwell, Victoria 3124, Australia
Penguin Books (Canada), 90 Eglinton Avenue, Suite 700, Toronto, Ontario, Canada M4P 2Y3
Penguin Books India Pvt Ltd, 11 Community Centre, Panchsheel Park, New Delhi - 110 017, India
Penguin Books (NZ) Ltd, 67 Apollo Drive, Mairangi Bay, Auckland 1310, New Zealand
Penguin Books (South Africa) (Pty) Ltd, 24 Sturdee Avenue, Rosebank, Johannesburg 2196, South Africa

Penguin Books Ltd, Registered Offices: 80 Strand, London WC2R 0RL, England